£20.00

MILITARY MOTORCYCLES OF WORLD WAR 2

OSPREY
COLLECTOR'S
LIBRARY

MILITARY MOTORCYCLES OF WORLD WAR 2

All makes from Europe, Russia, Japan and the USA 1939–1945

Roy Bacon

Published in 1985 by Osprey Publishing Limited
12–14 Long Acre, London WC2E 9LP
Member company of the George Philip Group

© Copyright Roy Bacon 1985

This book is copyrighted under the Berne Convention. All rights reserved. Apart from any fair dealing for the purpose of private study, research, criticism or review, as permitted under the Copyright Act, 1956, no part of this publication may be reproduced, stored in a retrieval system, or transmitted in any form or by any means, electronic, electrical, chemical, mechanical, optical, photocopying, recording, or otherwise, without prior written permission. All enquiries should be addressed to the publisher.

British Library Cataloguing in Publication Data

Bacon, Roy H.
   Military motorcycles of World War 2: all makes from Europe, Russia, Japan and the USA—1939 to 1945.—(Osprey collector's library series)
   1. Motorcycles—History   2. Vehicles, Military—History
   623.74′72   UC347
ISBN 0-85045-618-5

Editor Tim Parker
Filmset and printed in England by
BAS Printers Limited, Over Wallop, Hampshire

Contents

Acknowledgements 6

Outbreak 8

1 Austria and Puch 12

2 Belgium – three names predominate 20
FN/Gillet/Sarolea

3 Czechoslovakia – a curious tale 25

4 Denmark – the Nimbus Four 28

5 England – more makes than most 32
AMC/Ariel/BSA/Cotton/Douglas/James/Norton/Royal Enfield/Triumph/Velocette/Welbike

6 France – six makes or more 92

7 Germany – not just flat twins 96
Ardie/BMW/DKW/NSU/TWN/Victoria/Zundapp

8 Italy – war stopped the racing 128
Benelli/Bianchi/Gilera/Moto Guzzi/Volugrafo Aermoto

9 Japan – were they all copies? 142

10 Poland – the Sokol 146

11 Russia – some were home-made 149

12 Sweden – neutral but not inactive 153

13 Switzerland – an active industry 160

14 USA – 'the motorcycle that won the war' 161
Crosley/Cushman/Harley-Davidson/Indian/Simplex

Epilogue 179

Specifications 180

Acknowledgements

This book involved more people and more letter writing than any other I have ever written. Without their assistance it would never have been finished or have the content it has.

Collecting the information meant research into many sources and two of the most helpful were the National Motor Museum at Beaulieu and the Imperial War Museum who copied reports held in their outstation store for me. Companies still in existence and thought to have built military machines were contacted and information came from Batavus, BMW Munich, Fichtel & Sachs, Husqvarna, Jawa-CZ, Moto Guzzi, MZ, Steyr-Daimler-Puch and Zundapp. The last sent me a 300-page book on the company which detailed the many interesting and unusual models they have built.

Puch sent data, many pictures and replied to queries, MZ sent my letter on to the Zweitakt Motorradmuseum who replied with DKW photos and Moto Guzzi sent both data and pictures. From Peter Zollner of BMW came what I needed on both the flat twins and the upright singles. Stefan Knittel checked my German history. Husqvarna built no machines for the period but put me in touch with Harry Ljungdahl who has 4000 kg of m42 parts! He most kindly sent me much data on Swedish machines, checked the manuscript and risked being arrested taking photos of his machine near an army depot.

In Belgium Roland Servais did a similar job with that country's machines, and others in Europe who came to my assistance were Douglas Graham in Denmark, the late Erwin Tragatsch and Tjako Wolters.

At home friends made when writing earlier books rallied round and the AMC, Ariel, Royal Enfield and Velocette sections were checked respectively by Deryk Wylde, Jim Lee, Ivor Mutton and Ivan Rhodes. Other help came via the VMCC experts from Bill Hume, Mike Jackson and Peter Misaurio while Titch Allen and Bob Currie both helped with information on the Sunbeam, Bob also identifying some pictures for me.

New contacts made at home were Gerard Gilligan who offered me Gilera help, Harry Bullens who is the Welbike expert and Iain Cottrell with data and a photo of the V-twin Indian. Three Harley-Davidson enthusiasts also did their best for me; Jim Dowdall, Jim Hunt and Paul Parslow. Finally, I must thank Maurice Kelly who sorted out the Russian scene for me and corrected my scraps of inaccurate data from his immense store of Soviet machine knowledge.

For the pictures the aim was to use as many contemporary shots as feasible to try to give the flavour of the times when rationing, bombs and security ruled nearly all countries. Many such photos come stamped on the rear with a press agency, censor marks, British Official Photograph plus other notes gained over the past 40 years or so. We hope the selection sets the tone.

Many pictures came from either Beaulieu, Imperial War Museum or through the good offices of the EMAP archives which now hold the old *Motor Cycle Weekly* files. In many cases they are also marked with other sources so their origin is sometimes obscure. Some of these have been mentioned above and to the two English museums must be added the East German one, Zweitakt. Manufacturers who supplied pictures were BMW, Moto Guzzi, Steyr-Daimler-Puch and Zundapp.

Many of the pictures stamped British Official Photograph were sent out also marked by the agency who either took them or had the censor pass them. The firms involved in this activity included Associated Press, BIPPA, Fox Photos, International News Photo, Keystone Press Agency, London News Agency Photos, Photographic News Agencies, Planet News, Sport & General Press Agency and The 'Topical' Press Agency. The stamp of the *Daily Herald* also appears on one photo.

At an official level some pictures are marked Ministry of Information, the Australian equivalent and Ministère de l'Information while one was taken by Harrison Roberts, an accredited US army war correspondent. In the same class is maybe one by Jack Sands, USMC, Maryland.

The professional cameramen whose work is used are Bretislav Dmych of Prague, Knud Jorgensen of Denmark, Dominique Pascal of France, Alan Williams and Mick Woollett. Others who helped from their collections were Christopher Barbarski of the Sikorski Museum in London, Iain Cottrell, Bob Currie, Harry Ljungdahl, Ivor Mutton, Dick Platt from the VMCC photo library and Roland Servais.

To all who contributed in any way at all, my thanks and especially to Tim Parker who helped so much with this one.

Roy Bacon
Niton, Isle of Wight
February 1985

Outbreak

In the days of the gas scare, a rider rode with mask but no safety helmet. Note headlamp mask and map holder

Germany invaded Poland on 1 September 1939, and within days much of Europe was once more plunged into conflict. At first most people spoke of it all being over by Christmas, but behind the scenes authority knew that only the first skirmishes would take place in that time.

Few of those who had the real facts thought the struggle would drag on for six long, hard and grim years or that it would extend to affect just about every country on the globe in one way or another. But it did, and during those years the motorcycle played its part in all fields to carry messages, marshall convoys, transport officers, police troops and act as a mobile fighting unit.

The use of motorcycles and their form varied from country to country, with the English machines mainly simple singles, the German ones complex twins and the Americans rather large, rather heavy and mostly with V-twin engines.

They all played their part and after the war many ran on in a black civilian coat of paint to offer prosaic transport to the public. Hardly exciting, but available at a time when everything was in short supply.

No book of this size can hope to carry every single detail or development change even for those motorcycles used in World War 2. Each country's machines, even each machine type,

Taken in 1940 to hearten the public when events looked bad for England. Daylight raids made cover essential, hence the dome

The Local Defence Volunteers were formed in 1940 and later became the Home Guard. Here a unit construction, New Imperial, parades before HM King George VI

needs a book of its own to satisfy the inquisitiveness of some enthusiasts — there are no part numbers, no paint codes, no unit designations, nor even production figures within these pages.

In fairness, such is the complication of this subject, it's a whole new minefield when researching what military forces actually did to their motorcycles when in the field under fire, that we carry little 'fighting duties' information. Our aim has been to list, describe and illustrate what was factory built and used somewhere during the conflict of 1939 to 1945.

Typical line-up of men and machines ready to serve. Models are M20 BSA and the bald tyres pay their tribute to the rubber shortage

Outbreak

1 Austria and Puch

The end of World War 1 saw the break-up of the Austro-Hungarian empire and the establishment of several new countries, with Austria, Hungary, Czechoslovakia and Yugoslavia as separate states. Two decades later, in 1938, Austria and the Czechs found themselves annexed by Hitler and part of the new German empire.

The oldest and largest motorcycle firm in Austria was formed in 1934 from the amalgamation of Steyr, Austro-Daimler and Puch and in the matter of powered two-wheelers continued with the machines and designs of the latter. Puch machines dated from 1903 and in the period between the wars adopted the split single engine with great success.

From 1938 they were considered as part of the German industry and so came under the Schell plan for rationalization. With the need for more and more production the factory was kept busy producing machines for the Wehrmacht until 1942, when it was heavily bombed.

Three split single two-strokes were built over this period and another also saw some duty with the military as a conscript. Finally there was a large four-stroke built in limited numbers in the late thirties and intended for solo or sidecar army use.

The oldest design was that of the 250S4, which dated from 1934 and was itself based on the 1929 model T. The engine construction was unusual to say the least, but followed lines set down with

The Puch 200 cc split single with crankshaft along the frame. Pressed steel frame surrounds fuel tank. A conscript machine

the marque's first split single built in 1924. Thus it had the crankshaft set in line with the frame and the two pistons side by side across it. They shared a forked connecting rod, which served to give asymmetric timing for both exhaust and transfer ports, while the two cylinders kept clean new and dirty old gases apart. The theory was that once the plug had fired up in the single combustion chamber the pistons were driven down and as the ports opened fresh mixture purged up one cylinder and down the other.

It worked well and Puch were competitively successful up to 1931 with water-cooled and blown models. In 1934 the earlier road models were improved and the result was the 250S4. This had bores of 45 mm coupled to a 78 mm stroke to give a 248 cc capacity and the compression ratio was 6·5 : 1.

Engine construction was based on a vertically split crankcase, but with the joint running across

Military Motorcycles of World War 2

14

Left **An army padre with a captured Puch 250S4 in 1944 in Italy a few days before D-Day came many miles away**

Above **A restored model 350GS Puch with offset tandem piston engine, sometimes odd bore size and tension rear suspension springs**

the machine and not fore-and-aft as normal. The single-throw crankshaft carried generator and points for coil ignition at its front end and the crankcase was surmounted by the cast iron barrel and the separate head.

The single exhaust pipe came from the front left corner of the block and connected to a single silencer mounted low down on the same side. The carburettor was positioned behind the block and fed the inlet, which was at the left rear corner. The right cylinder provided the transfer porting.

Lubrication was very modern, with an oil pump set in the gearbox casting behind the barrel. It was supplied from a tank beneath the saddle and its output was varied by throttle control and fed into the inlet tract.

The unusual design extended past the engine to the transmission, for the four-speed gearbox was bolted to the rear of the crankcase and driven directly via a pair of bevel gears. These swung the axis of the shafts round so that a chain drive to the rear wheel could be used, but the clutch was not in the engine unit at all but in the rear hub.

The gearbox was conventional in layout but

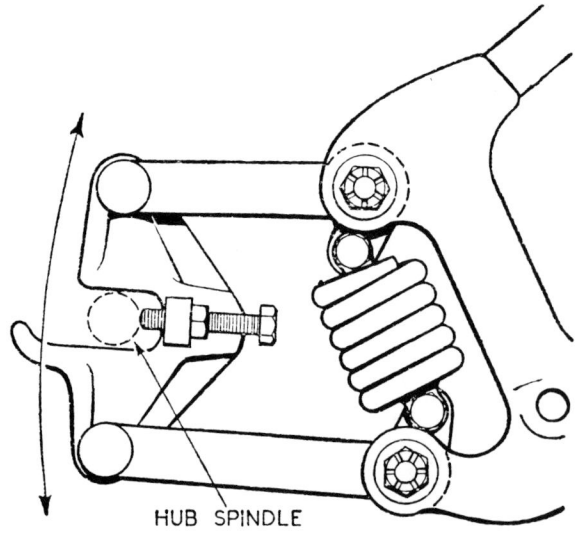

Interesting Puch rear suspension designed to give constant rear chain tension

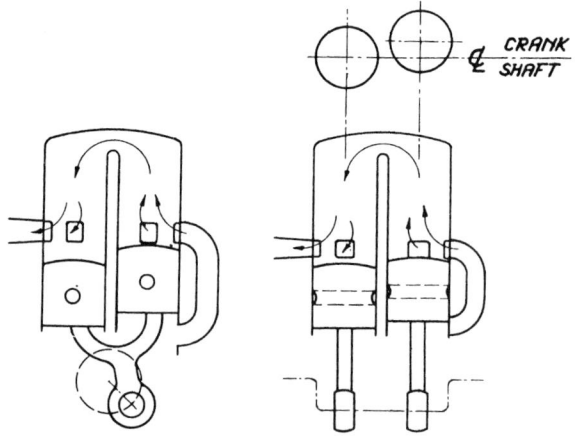

Puch layouts: left is 250S4 and right the offset 350GS. The 125 was similar to the 250 but with the engine turned in the frame.

modern in that its four ratios were all indirect. Its casing was split along the machine with shaft bearings in each side, and the open-front assembly bolted to the crankcase to mesh the bevels of the two units. Gear selection was by barrel cam with this turned by a rack and integral pinion. The rack was attached by rod to the hand change lever on the right side of the fuel tank.

The clutch went in the rear hub between it and the sprocket. It was a servo unit with a single central light spring backed up by weights which helped to clamp the plates under centrifugal loading. It did not make for good gear changes.

The cycle parts were more conventional with the unit construction, for that was what it was, engine and gearbox mounted in a tubular cradle frame with H-section down member. The rear

The Puch 250 and 350 gearbox, bevel driven directly from the crankshaft with rack and pinion to turn selector drum

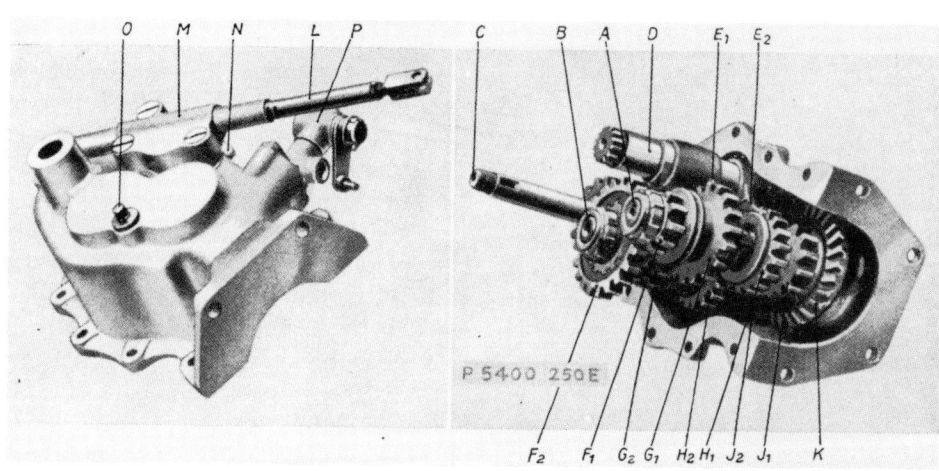

end was rigid and at first tubular girders were fitted. In 1935 these changed to pressed steel blades and with them came changes in the speedometer drive and front brake. The saddle springs and silencer also altered, but the tank (except for styling variations), toolbox and rear guard stayed as they were.

In 1938 the 250 was joined by the 350GS and this too was to find itself in the army in short order. It also had an odd engine and in some respects it was stranger than the 250. What it had in common with the smaller model was a crankshaft in line with the frame, a four-speed gearbox bolted directly to it and driven by bevel gears and a clutch in the rear hub. The two transmissions were in fact the same, although the overall gear ratio was raised for the larger model.

Internally the engine was a good deal different, for the cylinders were in tandem and each piston had its own rod running on a common crankpin. The split single effect of differential movement was obtained by staggering the two bores so they were not in line with one another.

The exhaust was at the front with a pipe and silencer on each side and each pipe was connected to two ports so the engine had four in all. Each exhaust system terminated in a high-level silencer. The single carburettor fed both bores and the transfer operation took place in the rear cylinder.

A further odd feature was that while the engine dimensions were normally quoted as 2 × 51·5 × 83·4 mm to give 347 cc, Puch data indicates that unequal bore sizes were also used. This and other sources give the rear transfer cylinder as 48 mm and the front one as 55 mm so the capacity came out as 349 cc. Even the big end had its points with the needle rollers it ran on held apart, not by a cage but by side washers with slots to engage with the needle ends. These washers were made in three sections for some reason.

To an extent the cycle parts were as for the 250 and the frame was again of the cradle type.

At the rear it had an unusual form of rear suspension with two unequal-length links carrying a member in which the rear wheel was mounted. The link movement ensured that the spindle moved in an arc centred on the gearbox sprocket and thus kept chain tension constant.

Each link was extended to form a bell crank and between the second arms went a tension spring to provide the suspension medium. A report written in late 1945 suggests that in military service the rear chain was liable to jump off the sprockets due to the suspension and for this reason the army kept to a rigid frame. It is true that the system relied on the rigidity of the wheel spindle in the fork ends to keep the wheel upright and on tracks the loading could have been too much for it.

At the front end went the blade girders of the 250 and for both models each blade was formed from two pressings welded together along their length. Two tension springs formed the suspension medium, and friction fork and steering dampers were fitted. Brakes were again single leading shoe drums operated by right hand and foot, while the kickstart lever was on the right as before.

The oil tank was a different shape but still tucked away under the seat behind the engine. The fuel tank was in two halves, each with its own filler cap, joined by a central strip above the frame top tube. It was thus as for the 250 and only differed in the lack of gear change gate on the right. For the 350 a footchange on the left was provided connected to the gearbox by several links, but as required by the German rules a hand change lever was also fitted.

The third split single came in 1939 and was of 125 cc capacity. It was far more modern in concept and had a conventional unit-construction engine incorporating a three-speed gearbox with a clutch on the end of the input shaft. As the box was of the all indirect type, and also with cross-over drive, the engine ran in the opposite sense to the road wheels but with its

Puch twin piston 125 of more conventional appearance and design

crankshaft axis across the machine.

This placed the cylinders one behind the other with the front having twin exhausts and an intake passage on the left, which was fed from a single carburettor behind the cylinder. A sports version had a different barrel that took a carburettor on each side on stubs which ran directly into the cylinder. The rear barrel had twin transfer ports.

The transmission was by chain on the left to the gearbox and on the right to the rear wheel. Thus the generator and points went on the right end of the crankshaft, while ignition was by coil powered from a battery carried under the cantilever sprung saddle. Lubrication was by petroil at 25:1, which simplified manufacture but was really a step back.

The frame was tubular and the forks simple blade girders with a compression spring. The rest of the cycle parts were basic but adequate, with lights, a toolbox, rear carrier and tyre pump completing a very useful lightweight.

Of the two conscripted models one was a 200 with much in common with the engine and transmission of the S4. Changes were to a shorter stroke to reduce the capacity, a lower compression ratio and only three speeds. The cycle parts differed with the frame built up from channel-section steel pressings, with the fuel tank set between the top members. Blade girders formed the only suspension and the details were common to the range.

The second model was very different and one of the few four-strokes made by Puch during its history after World War 1. The power unit was a sophisticated one which came into being in 1936. It was a flat four with side valves and a capacity of 792 cc. The carburettor sat above the crankcase to feed to each side and the exhausts ran from front and rear of each block to join at the silencer on either side of the machine. Lubrication was dry sump, with the oil tank under the saddle and ignition by coil. The generator went on the front of the engine and the camshaft above the crankshaft.

A four-speed gearbox was built in unit with the engine, but the clutch still went in the rear

The flat four Puch 800 with unit construction of side-valve engine and four-speed gearbox. Clutch remained in rear hub

hub and final drive was by chain on the left. The cycle parts were much as for the 250 but stretched to accommodate the longer engine. Thus the frame was a cradle with H-section down member and twin tubes bolted to its lower end and running back under the blocks. No rear suspension was provided and the blade girders went on the front. Both mudguards were well valanced, but in other details the big four used much from the two-strokes.

The techniques of building a flat four are very different to those for a split single and the 800 only stayed in production until 1938. Only 550 were built and many were intended for army use in either solo or sidecar form. The political annexation in 1938 brought the firm into the Schell programme and this dictated that Puch built 125 and 250 cc machines only. It could hardly have allowed the Austrians to have continued with a prestigious four alongside the Zundapp product, and by that time Puch had found that their model was not as good as it might have been.

So Puch continued with their split singles, at which they excelled, and the sanctions relaxed to allow the 350 to be built also until wartime production ceased.

2 Belgium – three names predominate

Of the many Belgian marques three predominate and all were situated in Herstallez-Liège, which was the centre of the country's motorcycle industry. All three were involved in the building of machines for the Belgian army, and following the occupation the production lines were kept going with forced labour.

FN

Fabrique Nationale d'Armes de Guerre was to Belgium what BSA was to England, a major armament firm who also dealt in motorcycles. The company dated from Edwardian times and was then best known for its in-line fours with shaft drive, built when the rest of the world travelled by belt.

For the Belgian army of the late 1930s FN produced another shaft-driven machine, but in this case the engine was a flat twin. It was a one-litre unit with side valves and was built in unit with the gearbox. A single carburettor fed both barrels and the manifold was embodied with the cover over the electrical equipment fitted on top of the crankcase. The timing gear went at the front and both exhausts went to a silencer on the right.

The frame was duplex, to fit round the engine unit, and fitted with girder front forks. The drive to the rear wheel was on the right of the machine, as was the sidecar, and from it a shaft drove the sidecar wheel also. The resulting perfor-

The massive FN with shaft drive to both rear and sidecar wheels

mance in the mud of Flanders so impressed the Germans, whose R12 models had severe traction problems, that they ordered a similar design for the Wehrmacht which resulted in the complex BMW and Zundapp machines.

The FN had massive section tyres with heavy treads fitted and carried a spare on the back of the sidecar body. This was large and heavily built on a loop chassis with tow-tube at the rear. Provision was made for mounting a machine gun on the front and rear decks and the outfit was generally larger than those used by other nations.

Construction of the whole machine was massive and crash and protection bars took care of the cylinder, on the left, and the driver or passenger.

FN also built a tricar using the flat twin M12 as a basis. To the motorcycle frame and front

end was attached an open body with two rows of seats. Two rear wheels on a car-type rear axle transmitted the drive as on the sidecar and a spare went on the back of the body. The gearbox contained four speeds and reverse and the intention was for the vehicle to operate in any conditions. As well as personnel it could also be used as an ammunition carrier. Postwar it became a delivery truck using a different frame.

Other FN models were used solo by the military, among them the M11, M71 and M86, and these came from the range of side and overhead valve singles produced by the firm. They were all of unit construction with chain final drive and conventional in form, but it is for the big flat twin that FN is best remembered in those years.

Gillet

For the army this company produced a big parallel twin, two-stroke-engined machine with sidecar. The idea of a two-stroke for this application was unusual at that time, except for DKW, but

Left **The FN tricar demonstrating how well it could cope with difficult conditions**

Below left **The Gillet with parallel twin two-stroke engine and same heavily built sidecar as all Belgian machines**

Below **A Sarolea with sidecar, not the flat twin but one of the singles and built to cope with army life**

the engine was large and tuned for low-down power.

Capacity was 708 cc and a 180-degree crankshaft was used. Construction was conventional, with vertical cylinders, carburettor at the rear and exhaust to the front with silencer on the right. The gearbox was built in unit with the engine and contained four speeds and reverse. It drove the rear wheel by chain and from this a shaft took the drive across to the sidecar wheel.

The remainder of the machine was conventional, with a tubular and rigid frame, girder forks and the usual cycle parts. The sidecar, as used by FN and Sarolea, was designed more for military use than its aesthetics and carried the inevitable spare wheel on its back panel.

After the war the model was also used by the police, but seemingly in smaller numbers than the four-strokes built by other firms.

As in other countries some of the civilian machines were called to the colours, and models that served included a 175 cc two-stroke and side valve singles from 350 to 600 cc.

Sarolea

This, the third of the Belgian big three, produced a range of four-stroke singles in the late 1930s. These were from 350 to 600 cc in capacity and each model was produced with side or overhead valves. Construction was conventional with separate four-speed gearboxes and the cycle side a rigid frame with girder forks. Some of these were used by the army as conscripts.

For the military, Sarolea built a sidecar outfit very similar to the FN. Like it the machine was massive and again it was propelled by a one-litre flat twin engine with side valves. Engine construction was very similar and in the gearbox went three speeds and reverse plus a dual-range box. This gave the driver a total of six forward and two reverse gears so he had a good chance of coping with all conditions.

Shaft drive was again used and carried across to the sidecar wheel, and there can be no doubt that the Belgians took the problems of finding traction in mud very seriously. The wheels were shod with the same heavy-section and well-treaded tyres and a spare was carried. Even if the outfit stuck, all was not lost as the sidecar wheel had a cable drum winch built into it. Thus the driver could find a tree, hook up the cable and pull himself out of the mire.

The frame was much as the FN, fitted with girder forks and massive enough to cope with arduous conditions and heavy-booted soldiers. The sidecar itself was as used by FN and was no doubt common, as were many of the minor details.

In all a tough machine and again one that impressed the Germans with its efficiency when the going got really bad.

3 Czechoslovakia – a curious tale

1945 and the 250 Jawa makes its debut having been developed behind *entry verboten* **doors under the Germans' noses**

The last chapter of Hitler's *Mein Kampf* is called 'What is necessary is right', and the German annexation of the Czech country was carried out on that basis. Expansion to the south-east along the Danube to the Ukraine and the Balkans would still the fears of the west while providing a rich harvest; but Czechoslovakia stood in the way and so had to go.

The army's motorcycles were by then rather prosaic, but in the 1920s the Czechs had some of the best racing models of the time at their disposal. Most came from England and they ranged in size from 250 cc to a big V-twin Brough Superior. This all came about because the army officer in charge of the purchasing was a racing enthusiast and, as could be expected, the ministry men who paid the bills had no idea that the money was for TT racers and not sturdy plodders.

Naturally it was the same officer who rode the Brough to many race victories, with the other machines also having many successes. It was really just too good to last, of course, and a scandal in 1929 brought the happy circus to an end.

Within a year or two the general unrest in Europe and the rise of the Nazi party ensured that military expenditure went up rather than down, but on the motorcycle front this need was now met by sturdy, reliable but boring machines from the home factories. A few machines still came from abroad, with Indian and BSA V-twins

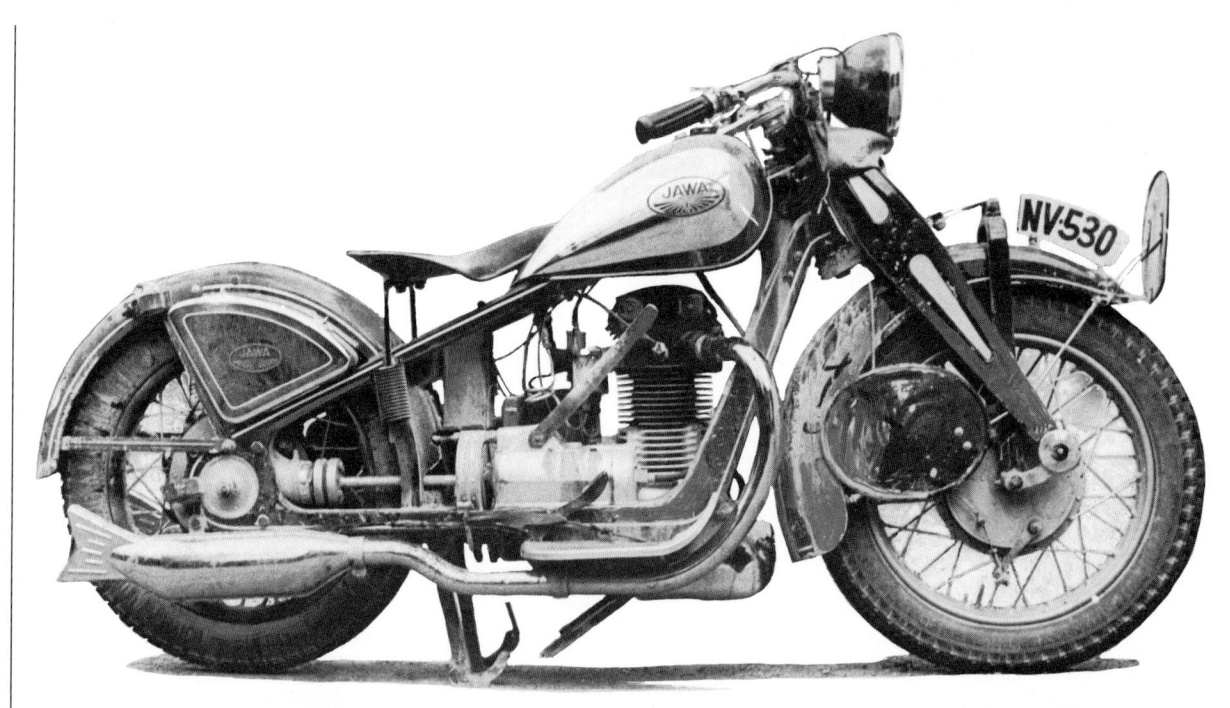

Military Motorcycles of World War 2

26

Left **The Jawa 500 used by the army with overhead valves, shaft drive and pressed steel frame**

Below left **The postwar Ogar, a marque taken over by Jawa, and a neat machine for the period**

plus BSA singles being used.

From the home factories came some rather conventional machines, but Jawa, one of the best known, was kept on motorcycle repairs for the Germans during the war. Under the occupiers' noses the firm also designed and developed a new 250 cc two-stroke single engine and gearbox unit for postwar use. Much of this took place in a shed marked 'secret – entry verboten'. It was so secret that none of the Germans knew what went on in it.

Among the prewar range was a 500 single and this was taken up by the army. It had overhead valves, unit construction, shaft drive and a pressed steel frame in the fashion of many European firms of that period. The front forks were trailing link with leaf spring at one time but later changed to girders.

Postwar the Jawa marque took over the Ogar factory and the 350 twin was at first sold under that label. Prewar Ogar mainly built a nice 250 cc two-stroke single with a sports line and performance. With them came the Premier 500 cc side-valve single and 750 cc V-twin, the latter used with a sidecar. Another V-twin came from the Walter firm, but in this case the engine was installed transversely with the gearbox in unit but with chain final drive.

In the earlier thirties the Itar flat twin of 750 cc was used with the cylinders fore and aft, the gearbox tucked in behind and an all-chain drive. It was more of a vintage design than from the thirties but was used by the army. The Praga was the BD with a new name and styled more from the thirties with a pressed steel frame. The engine was a 500 cc single with overhead camshaft built in unit with the gearbox and driving the rear wheel by shaft.

Finally there was Ceska Zbrojovka, another arms factory like BSA or FN. From CZ came a line of two-stroke singles and twins in pressed steel frames with girder forks. Sizes ranged up to 500 cc, a twin, and their construction was in the European style with the tank set in between the frame top tubes.

4 Denmark – the Nimbus Four

It took the German Blitzkrieg just one short day to over-run small, flat, peaceful Denmark. The day was 9 April 1940, and from then on the Danes were there to produce bacon and butter for the Nazis' breakfast.

On the motorcycling front just one make and model was taken up by the army, the Nimbus Four; built by Fisker and Nielsen of Copenhagen. The firm was unique in that over its years of production, first from 1919 to 1928 and then from 1934 to 1958, it built just one model, and the first was to the same general specification as the last.

The basis of the machine was an in-line four-cylinder engine with shaft drive to the rear wheel. The early machines had inlet over exhaust valves, girders and a spring frame. This last was again odd in that it was made from flat steel strip; the tank was welded to it and so was part of the structure, an early monocoque in embryo.

The 1934 model was different. The engine now had an overhead camshaft, which was shaft driven from the front. The vertical shaft was also the dynamo armature, just as on MG cars of the period, and a line of rockers poked out of each side of the camshaft housing. They operated exposed valves set either side of the combustion chamber and stayed that way to the end. The ignition distributor went on the front of the camshaft.

One carburettor went on the left of the engine, its small size restricting the power to

The Nimbus four with sidecar and light machine gun plus ammunition boxes

Military Motorcycles of World War 2

30

Left **Nimbus with sidecar well loaded with 20 mm ammunition. Note telescopic forks on this prewar model**

Below left **20 mm cannon on Nimbus sidecar outfit. Quite a heavy gun for such a platform**

22 bhp from the 750 cc capacity. The exhausts joined on the right and a pipe ran from the rear of the manifold down to the silencer. Its poor style and line matched the rest of the machine, which was a bizarre combination of the modern and the antique.

The clutch and three-speed gearbox bolted to the rear of the engine. Gear changing was by hand, with the lever emerging at the rear of the tank, although later models were fitted with footchange. Starting was by a transverse pedal on the left and the final drive by exposed shaft and bevels. The lubrication of these was extremely crude and they had to manage with some grease at service time. The valve stems were looked after in the same casual manual way, but the lubrication system was a high-pressure, wet sump type to suit the plain bearing crankshaft with its two mains. The gearbox was lubricated from the engine via the clutch shaft.

The Nimbus frame continued in flat strip but became rigid at the rear. At the front went telescopic forks, so the marque may well have preceded the much more publicized BMW as the first in the world to offer this feature.

The wheels were conventional with drum brakes while the tank fitted between the top frame members. Saddle and pillion seat were sprung using rubber loops at the rear mounting until rubber went into short supply and then normal springs were used. On some models the front mudguard was very heavily valanced, and the Danish Red Cross used it to take the traditional marking on their all-white machines.

Postwar the four continued with only minor changes, but the firm also built prototypes with rotary valves. The first was a four that worked well and was followed by a tandem twin, but neither went into production as the firm decided to stop motorcycle manufacture.

5 England – more makes than most

Lovely period advertisement taken from *Motor Cycling* in July 1945

When Neville Chamberlain spoke to the British people on 3 September 1939 they once again found themselves engaged in a war for which they were ill-prepared. It was to prove fortunate for the country that a few long-sighted industrialists had seen the way the wind was blowing some years earlier and had taken steps to ensure the people had a measure of protection. To achieve this they worked in the face of Government indifference, but thanks to their determination and commitment the country had Hawker Hurricane aircraft and BSA guns, among other items, to meet the enemy with in the early dark days.

It was the same with motorcycles. During the 1930s the peace-time experts at the War Office dabbled with a 500 cc V-twin of some complexity. It was not until 1937 that it became accepted that in wartime a tough, simple machine is essential. Tough to withstand service use with minimal maintenance and simple so it was cheap and hence disposable without heartache. By 1940 they knew their decision was right as the army no longer had the leisure or tools needed for a more complex machine. Simplicity paid off in battle when the rider had to improvise or walk. Most were allergic to the latter so would find a way to persuade the model home.

During the thirties Gilbert Smith of Nortons played his part. He had a factory racing team travelling around Europe to feed him information and from this could see the conflict coming and with it a huge demand for transport. He wanted a good slice of this business for his company as he considered this a better use of their assets than for them to make anonymous parts as a munitions factory.

To this end he cultivated the purchasing departments and selected army officers. The latter were asked to attend events such as the ISDT and the TT, and the firm would aid their enjoyment by preparing their reports.

So under pressure from both BSA and Norton the War Office moved away from the complex to the simple single that these two firms were to build in bulk. They were supported by a number of others and backed by a few ultra-lightweights. These were propelled by the two-stroke engine hated by the service chiefs but dictated by the needs of the machine. In truth they worked well for the airborne troops and most of the models were built with little change throughout the war years.

The War Office issued contracts for machines in 1937 and a new military specification in 1938. When the war began the delivered supplies fell far short of the immediate needs and the new models were barely into prototype form. To deal with the first problem the authorities simply impounded everything they fancied, mainly from the makers, but also from some dealers.

This meant that some were 1940 models not yet in the showrooms. The industry traditionally switched production after the work's fortnight holiday to build up stocks ready for the show in November. This process had already begun, so army riders became the first to sample some of the new models. All were made to look much the same by simply standing them in front of a wall and aiming a spray gun at them. All were painted khaki and were done as they stood, tyres, seat, the lot. Once painted they blended in fairly well with the 'real' army machines, for these still had kneegrips, handlebar rubbers and footrests among less essential comforts soon to be left off.

From the War Office specification came the very light Triumph 3TW, but plans to build this on a massive scale were destroyed in the Coventry blitz. Many motorcycle factories were bombed at that time, which, taken with the equipment lost at Dunkirk, placed the emphasis on production only.

So the English motorcycle fought its war with little change in the main although innovations came. The Matchless turned to teles, the Welbike was developed for paratroops, and lightweights also found themselves falling out of planes with just a silk parachute and a tube frame to keep them straight and narrow. For the rest it was thousands upon thousands of singles that simply plodded about their business.

Towards the end of the war the Ministry of Supply decided it was time to think again and a new specification was issued, based on the experiences of the services in all the theatres of war. This called for two cylinders and side valves,

The Don R at rest in his barrack as seen through official army eyes with all his kit clean and squared away

a fully enclosed transmission system, minimal controls in a standard pattern and low weight, the aim being 300 lb. Maximum speed was to be between 60 and 70 mph and fuel consumption over 80 mpg on a 100-mile circuit covered at a 30 mph average. It had to climb a 1 in 2·24 test hill at a steady 4 mph and restart on the same gradient, accelerate smoothly from 10 mph in top gear, average 45 mph over a standing quarter and be inaudible at half a mile range. For cross-country work it had to keep running in 15 in. of water and have 6 in. of ground clearance. BSA, Douglas and Triumph all built machines to conform to this specification but only the last ever reached production, in a modified form, and mainly went to forces overseas, although the RAF used some.

So the English ran true to form, being poorly prepared at the start, suffering reverses at early stages, doggedly struggling through with gritted teeth and barely suitable equipment and producing the real tool for the job after it was all over.

In addition to the larger singles the services also bought a number of 250 cc machines and these were used for training, liaison work and for use by the ladies of the three arms of the forces.

Typical army exercise for its dispatch riders with the sergeant about to help vocally to pick the machine up

The numbers of such models were smaller and they were kept away from war zones to avoid spares and service support problems that might otherwise have arisen.

When the war came to its end the army found itself with far more machines than it needed so large numbers were sold off. It took some prodding before this happened, and at first machines were stored in open-air dumps and riders thought they would be able to visit these, make their choice and pay for it. In practice the machines were sold in large lots to those dealers with the initiative to buy them up.

In many cases the machines were fully overhauled before release as such work kept the army workshops busy while awaiting demob. They retained the army colour, but as the public had had enough of khaki and olive green most dealers repainted them as a sales point. Black or maroon were the most common colours used and the ex-War Department motorcycle filled a very real gap on the home market in those post-war years.

The public was in dire need of transport and most of the new machines produced were destined for export to help the balance of payments. The service machines filled that gap and

35

had the advantages of being known, being available and being backed with many tons of spares.

Thousands of machines finished their days in mundane fashion, often towing a chair, until they were discarded for something better. Many had a more sporting existence and went on to be turned into specials for trials, scrambles or grasstrack, some even went to short-circuit racing.

AMC

The Matchless 350 was a very popular machine with the services from 1941 onwards when it gained its telescopic front forks. Prior to then it was in some ways even more desirable, for it was faster and really little removed from a late-type civilian sports single.

During the war years the Woolwich firm produced some 80,000 machines, and nearly all were built in the Matchless form with only a few AJS versions appearing early on. In real terms the only difference was the magneto position – ahead of the cylinder for AJS and behind for Matchless – and for spares holding it was no doubt thought best to stick with one type.

Anyone who has ever had to remove the dynamo from a Matchless single will know the trauma involved, but no doubt the War Office experts thought it best to keep the magneto out of harm's way. Maybe dynamo changing was thought to be good for the military soul if made excruciatingly awkward as only AMC could do.

The early model was the G3 and this used the well-tried single-cylinder ohv engine of 69 × 93 mm dimensions and 348 cc capacity. In AJS form it was the model 16, but effectively the same thing. The motor was very traditional in its build, with vertically split crankcase, iron head and barrel, built-up crankshaft with roller big end and timing gear on the right.

The cams were gear driven and a pair of pushrod tubes ran up from the crankcase to the cylinder head and the fully enclosed valve gear.

The exhaust valve lifter went in the timing case. The inlet camshaft on the Matchless and exhaust one on the AJS drove the magneto by chain inside a cover; when light alloy was in short supply the outer lid was cast in iron for a while.

An Amal carburettor was used along with dry sump lubrication, with the oil carried in a tank under the saddle on the right and circulated by a pump set in the timing case and driven from the crankshaft. Primary drive was by chain enclosed in the impossible AMC chaincase with the dynamo set behind the crankcase in the engine plates and also chain driven from the crankshaft. Access was limited.

The gearbox was a Burman with four speeds and footchange, both gear and kickstart pedals being on the right as usual on English machines. It and the engine went into a rigid frame with girder forks and this ran on wire-spoked wheels with single leading-shoe drum brakes.

The rest of the machine conformed to English and military standards of the times. Two toolboxes were fitted, one between the chainstays on the right and the other above it, while the rider travelled on a saddle with a rear carrier behind him. Front and rear stands were provided, the speedometer was fork mounted and frontwheel driven while the headlight was masked.

Behind this prosaic model lay some years of tests and a limited acceptance. The G3 had first gone to the army for evaluation in 1933, when its performance was commended as the best 350 and as good as the 500 cc Norton. At back of this the details were less encouraging, with various points adversely commented on. As the tests continued and the miles mounted up other faults appeared in the engine: in the valve gear, piston and big end.

A further test over 5000 miles was carried out on a 1936 G3 and a batch of 110 models bought, followed by the purchase of another 11, which were modified to an extent. Other orders followed, but only for a few machines at a time, until 1940, when the G3 War Office model was in its final form. By then the cylinder head had been changed from the Matchless type with hairpin valve springs to the AJS one with coil springs and rocker box caps over the valves.

The frame was that announced for the 1940 model range. It differed in that it had a single front down tube in place of the splayed pair that had passed either side of the crankcase. The tanktop panel went, of course, but the poor army rider was confused by a handbook showing the prewar details on his lubrication chart.

The G3 ran on into 1942 with the last batch built with telescopic forks, but before then the firm made other attempts to win a good-sized motorcycle contract. Popular rumour had it that they were crossed off the list because their factory was next door to Woolwich Arsenal and so certain to be bombed. On a more official basis the suggestion was that their machines were too heavy.

To meet this criticism and to fulfil the needs of the early War Office specification AMC submitted a pair of 250s. These were tested against other machines pared down below a 300 lb requirement and performed as well on paper but

Assembling Matchless G3 machines for the army early in 1940 at the AMC works

Military Motorcycles of World War 2

not really as well on the ground. The performance was there alright, but it came from a 7:1 compression ratio, very light flywheels and a power curve that peaked at 6000 rpm.

The sporty character meant insufficient torque at low speed, and it was soon found that the engine needed regular attention to maintain the performance. The army concluded that 350 cc was the minimum capacity to get the needed performance coupled with pulling power and the ability to thrive on neglect.

Left **Matchless G3 with small army headlamp and rear convoy light. A quick machine for keeping the trucks in line**

Below left **G3 line-up in the desert with the machines showing signs of use. Note side-arm worn on left hip**

Below **Happy is the corporal issued with a G3L with telescopic forks – unless the dynamo needs changing**

AMC trailed off and designed the G3L, the L reputedly standing for lightweight ... and then Coventry was bombed. Overnight the plans for a single special design went and the only need was for production, so the Plumstead works at last received its big service contracts.

The G3L was much as the G3 but with a lighter engine and frame. The design and construction were on the same lines and were to run on for many years after the war without much major change. The telescopic front forks proved to work well and were popular with riders. The spares for them provided forks postwar for many a competition machine as they were strong, well

Catch 22 **with a toolbox. The handbook with this diagram is the first item to be packed**

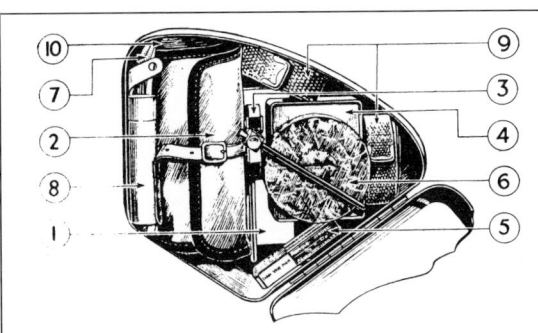

Illustration 21

Showing tools and equipment correctly stowed in tool box.

PACK, IN NUMERICAL ORDER, IN POSITIONS INDICATED.

(1) Driver's Handbook.
(2) Tool Bag.
(3) Chain Rivet Extractor.
(4) Tyre Repair Outfit.
(5) Rear Chain Spares.
(6) Insulating Tape.
(7) Tyre Levers. (2 Off).
(8) Tyre Pressure Gauge.
(9) Webbing Straps. (2 Off).
(10) Coil of Wire.

Right **Happiness is a ride over and a cup of char. In fact the rider is from the RAF Regiment and as it is Italy in 1944 he drinks coffee**

Below **The G3L with prototype rear suspension using rear units based on the front Teledraulics**

AMC V-twin prototype built in 1942 with 990 cc engine driving four-speed gearbox into forward and reverse box. Optional sidecar wheel drive which could be used on the road. AMC owned Sunbeam at the time. Driver is Jim Hall, first VMCC president with Harvey Pascoe in chair

damped and had light alloy lower legs.

The machine was quick enough to be able to cope with convoy duty, where it had to leap-frog the trucks to the next junction, and fast work was made exciting by the small diameter of the drum brakes.

In 1944 the G3L was used as a basis for a prototype with rear suspension, the rear units being adaptations of the front Teledraulic fork legs. That model was fitted with the AJS-style engine with front magneto and also sported a saddle whose single spring lived in the seat tube. With a fishtail silencer and laid-down units it looked rather Velocette, but the rear fork pivot design did reach the public in 1949. Until then AMC continued with the basic G3L and at the close of hostilities just changed the finish to black and built it and the equivalent 500 cc single under both AJS and Matchless badges.

In addition to their work with the G3L, AMC were also involved with the V-twin powered sidecar prototype built to replace the Norton Big 4. This appeared with Sunbeam transfers on the tank as AMC had acquired that concern pre-war, when the name of AMC was first coined, although they sold it on to BSA during the war.

The outfit was built in 1942 and was driven by a 990 cc ohv V-twin Matchless engine with single carburettor in the vee and twin exhaust pipes connecting to a single silencer mounted high on the right. Ignition was by a forward mounted magneto, the dynamo went above the gearbox and lubrication was dry sump.

The engine was housed in a very sturdy cradle frame with plenty of ground clearance and fitted with special heavyweight Teledraulics. It drove to a special four-speed gearbox which had a supplementary box to give the choice of forward or reverse. In theory at least the machine could run back as fast as forward but in practice the steering proved odd.

From the gearbox a chain drove the rear wheel and this in turn could be connected or not to drive the sidecar wheel. Unlike the Norton this outfit could be driven on the road with the drive engaged. For the rest the outfit sat on massive knobbly tyres and carried a four gallon petrol tank.

The gearing kept the cruising speed down to the forties and anything over 50 called for an excess of engine revs. Possibly to help in the mud and to inhibit soldiers unused to a performance outfit but irksome to those who knew the engine could have pulled it along at 75.

Following tests of the outfit, AMC received an order for a batch but could not cope with it as they were fully committed on the single. So the order went to the Standard car firm but was never fulfilled as the Jeep was preferred.

The prototype was in use for a decade after the war, mainly with a standard chair, and was then broken up. The top half of the engine converted a Brough SS80 into an SS100 and the bottom half went into another Brough. The frame was cut up and used as garage drive hardcore.

Thus ended the English attempt to build an

Above The 1939 Ariel 250 cc model OG, very similar to the 350 and seen here with wartime headlamp mask

Above right The 500 cc side-valve VA of which a small batch were made for the army early in the war

Below right The wartime Ariel, the W/NG. Other versions had a different upper toolbox with medial hinge

all terrain sidecar and they kept to lighter machines and the Jeep. As the Germans were to do in the end.

Ariel

The Ariel solution to the needs of the services was straightforward and simple. They took their standard 350, increased the ground clearance, deleted some of the more fragile items and gave it the mandatory drab olive finish of the army.

The result was typed the W/NG and was based largely on the competition derivative of the standard road NG. It was designed by Val Page on his return to the Ariel factory in the middle of 1939; he picked up from where he had left off after his years with the company from 1925 to 1932.

A prototype was very quickly built up and shown to the military men. The first to react were the French, who ordered a batch. These were duly sent on their way early in 1940. In the ensuing struggle they became forgotten and spent the next five years in a warehouse in Ostend, unpacked, unnoticed and unused. After the war they were returned to England and sold off as war surplus.

The engine was essentially the peacetime NG with its soft valve timing and a modest 6·5:1 compression ratio. The construction was standard English with vertically split crankcase and iron top half, timing gear on the right with pushrods to the overhead valves and chain drive up to the mag-dyno. It produced a modest 17 bhp at 5800 rpm and was a very tough unit indeed.

The primary drive retained the typical Ariel dry clutch, which lived in a separate compartment in the chaincase under a detachable outer dome, with an extra plate added to improve grip and life. The case continued in light alloy for some while, but, when this material fell into short supply and went mainly to the aircraft industry, Ariel changed to a pressed steel chaincase cover and did the same thing for the timing cover.

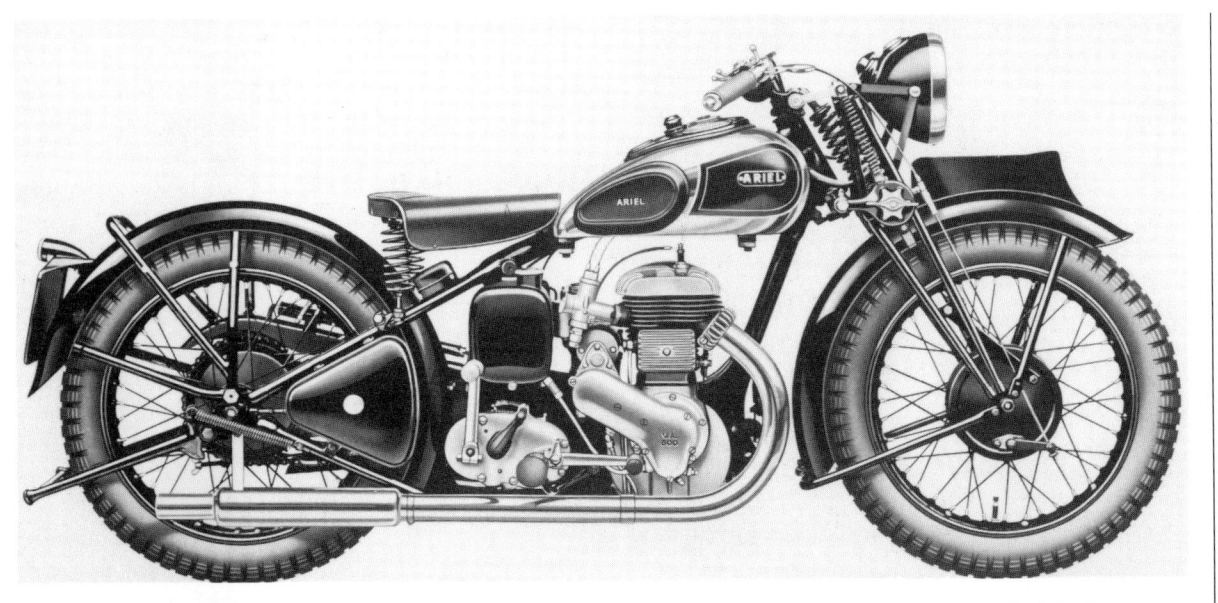

A four-speed Burman gearbox with foot-change was fitted, but in time this too gave up its light alloy and had a cast iron shell and end covers. For service use the speedometer drive was deleted from the box and the rollers in which the selector drum turned were changed for a bronze bush. The ratios were also special to the

A wartime Ariel advertisement taken from *The Motor Cycle* **of March 1941 and showing a nice blend of nostalgia and patriotism**

army and wider spaced than usual.

The frame was based on the standard rigid one with the rear sub-frame altered to lower the wheel and a lug added on the left by the saddle spring. This supported a very long prop stand with spike end, this formidable anchor stowing against the upper chain stay when not in use. A rear stand was also fitted. The forks were girders extended to increase the ground clearance with the aid of the lower rear end. (A postwar bonus was that the Ariel telescopic fork would fit straight into place.) The main central fork spring was of barrel form to give a variable rate and was assisted by two auxiliary springs, one on each side. Friction dampers were used for both the fork action and the steering.

At first the handlebars continued to be rubber mounted but after a few instances of them turning when used on the rough, normal clamps were adopted. Most of the detail fittings came from the civilian models, so the battery went on the left and the oil tank on the right. Two toolboxes were fitted, both on the right, and the lower was the stock one between the chainstays. Above it went another and this differed in that the lid hinged across the middle of the box so the contents had a chance of staying put when it was opened.

The instrument panel went from the petrol tank so the speedometer was mounted on the top of the forks on the right driven from a gearbox attached to the front brake backplate on that side. The ammeter was retained and went in front of the lighting switch in a small panel set in the headlamp shell, a standard Lucas arrangement.

The switch had four working positions labelled OFF, T, L and H for off, tail only, pilot and tail, and headlight. No dipswitch was fitted, but a twin filament headlamp bulb was installed, only wired to one side. Lighting was in truth a real problem for service riders, as on convoy runs they were expected to use the very small tail light only and on other duties the headlamp beam was severely curtailed by a mask.

With no instrument panel there was no place for the oil pressure gauge, so that went and at first a pressure regulator was fitted. From 1941 this too went and a spring-loaded ball valve was added behind the oil pump.

The machines were built in standard service format, which meant no rear number plate, a pillion seat and rests without rubbers and provision for the standard pannier frames and their canvas bags. A rear carrier straddled the frame behind the pillion seat and increased the model's carrying capacity.

The bulk of Ariel wartime production was the W/NG model and it served well, especially in forward areas, where its competition ancestry showed through. With good ground clearance it was able to cope with rough ground in some style, even if this biased the handling away from total precision on the road. On tarmac it was acceptable rather than good, but for all that could produce good cross-country averages.

Top speed was just over 70 mph, as one would expect from the power produced, so it could cruise happily at 55 mph. The big Ariel brakes adopted in 1926, and little altered in basic design some 30 years later, hauled the machine to a standstill at a rate more dependant on tyre grip than anything else. Fuel consumption usually bettered 80 mpg, so a tank of petrol gave it a decent operating radius. . . . A nice machine to draw from stores.

Ariel also produced 250 and 500 cc military

A 1941 picture of Home Guard forces on duty with Ariel combination and Lewis gun. Was the drum loaded? Would vibration set it firing?

In flight, in training. This Ariel has the more usual toolbox and was a tough motorcycle

machines in smaller numbers. The first were built in 1943 and followed the lines of the 350 very faithfully. In fact the only real change was the capacity, and this came from decreasing the bore to 61 mm and keeping the 85 mm stroke of the 350. In other respects it copied the larger model, as would be expected. Over 6000 of them were built and they went to all three services for use in most theatres of war.

In the same way the 500 cc machine used the W/NG cycle parts, but was powered by the side-valve VA engine. The model carrying this typing had been introduced to the range in 1939 to offer the slogging, low-down side-valve power desired by sidecar owners in a smaller class than the 600 cc model VB. This helped a little with insurance costs and put the marque back into direct competition with many other companies building similar machines.

In September 1939 the company found itself with some 100 VA engines surplus to needs, so set to and persuaded the Ministry that a small batch of W/VA models would help the war effort and could be produced quickly and easily. So they did just that, and despite the longer 95 mm stroke of the larger engine the crankcase dropped straight into the frame. The side-valve engine had no trouble fitting under the top tube and the rest of the machine was simply as used for the 350.

There was never any point in building more, with BSA and Norton both producing large numbers of 500 cc side-valve models, but at the time an extra 100 machines built quickly were well worth having.

So the Ariel contribution was one tough ohv built in quantity, a similar but smaller model and a handful of stock bin specials.

BSA

Birmingham Small Arms was a very large industrial firm that had been founded on the production of guns. It became involved with bicycles in 1880 as a means of diversification and for some time oscillated between the two products depending on the needs of the British Army and the desire to keep the workforce employed.

In 1910 they moved, perhaps inevitably, into the motorcycle field with a machine that was to become typical of their designs. It was straightforward, up-to-date, without any really unusual features, well made and well finished. This was a formula that seldom drew the headlines but always sold well and it kept the company solvent for some 60 years.

In 1914 BSA went to war and produced enormous numbers of guns, many thousands of folding bicycles and motorcycles for the armies of England, France and Russia. After it was over they consolidated their light engineering front by amalgamations with steel and tooling firms and concentrated their efforts on two-wheelers.

The gun plant stood idle for many years, but the BSA directors kept it in order, although it was 1935 before it was used again. A little earlier, in 1932, the War Office showed some signs of interest in two-wheeled transport and from discussions came an order to develop a 500 cc V-twin machine. This was duly done and numbers were then built for both the army and the RAF, while BSA capitalized on their work to produce the J model for sale to the public.

In 1937 there was a change of personnel at the War Office and with this a change of mind to the simple side-valve single. From BSA this meant the 500 cc M20 plus some of the newly introduced 250 cc C10 models for training purposes.

The M20 had been part of a new range of singles designed by Val Page when he joined the company in 1936. In one move he took the machines from a post-vintage style and specification to one that was to run into the 1960s. There were a dozen models in the line-up but all came from one design in two weights, the B for the lighter or sporty end of the market and the M for heavy-duty work.

The M20 thus used the heftier frame, forks and gearbox with a beefier bottom end for the engine. All models had one feature in common, which was the low-set oil pump with its attendant bulge in the base of the crankcase and consequent kink in the lower frame tube to run round it.

The engine construction was standard English for the period, with built-up flywheels, roller big end, vertically split crankcase and timing gear on the right. The valves were lifted by separate cams, each driven by gear from the crankshaft, and from the inlet gear an idler meshed with the mag-dyno gear. The oil pump was driven from a skew gear on the crankshaft and was a duplex gear unit to suit the dry sump system.

Head and barrel were in iron, with the sparking plug mounted above the inlet valve and the tappet adjusters under a small alloy cover fixed to a chamber cast into the side of the cylinder. A fifth cylinder-base nut went between the valves under the cover, with the exhaust valve lifter arm ahead of the cylinder.

The electrics were the inevitable Lucas mag-dyno held down by straps, with the dynamo readily detachable by itself. The control unit went on the rear mudguard under the saddle and the battery on the left to balance the oil tank on the right.

An immobilizer went into the high tension lead from the magneto to the plug. In use it was simply unscrewed with the plug lead and carried away, the lead left was then too short to reach the plug.

An Amal 276 carburettor of one-inch bore supplied the mixture with a separate float chamber on the right fed from twin taps situated at the rear of the tank on both sides. No air cleaner was fitted as standard, but this was not good enough when the machine was used in the western desert.

Under those conditions an air filter was necessary to cope with airborne grit and an essential if the model was dropped onto its right side. With the carburettor biased out rather than in it would take in handfuls of sand if unprotected and this could wreck the internals in a very short time indeed.

To deal with this a special Vokes air cleaner was attached to the top of the tank by straps

Right **Line-up of New Zealand signals men in training on M20 models**

Below right **No crash helmets then either. An Indian dispatch rider on an M20 in a trial held in Cyprus in 1942. Such events toned up riding skills in the fullest sense**

An M20 engine test bed rigged up in a workshop to check units before rebuilding into a machine

England – more makes than most

In the army you cope even if this means acting as ferryman to a BSA whose rider leaves the rowing to others

similar to those used for mag-dyno clamping. These were joined by screws to plates held by the kneegrip fixing. The air cleaner was of rectangular form with an intake grille with mesh in each side and an outlet tube at the right rear corner. This aimed the air down and was connected to the carburettor by a simple moulded hose. To enable this to reach its destination without impeding the rider the right rear corner of the petrol tank was cut away to a point level with the front end of the saddle nose recess. This gave room for the hose, although it still meant that the whole contraption was something of a nuisance to the rider.

The exhaust pipe was a push fit into the cylinder and was clipped to the frame. It terminated in a cylindrical silencer, which was tilted up a little so that its outlet was a little higher than on civilian models.

The transmission was stock M20 with engine shaft shock absorber, multi-plate clutch and single-strand primary and final drive chains. The first lived in a pressed steel chaincase with the outer half secured by innumerable small set screws. The latter was protected by guards on each run, although these were of little use in desert conditions and chains suffered accordingly.

The clutch was the type used by BSA up to 1936 for standard models and ran dry. To achieve this a pressed steel dome was secured to the chainwheel by a ring of small screws and a gasket. Under it went the pressure plate and behind that the clutch plates, with a total of eight fabric rings interleaved with metal plates splined alternately to clutch hub and drum. A single massive centre spring applied the clamping pressure and was compressed by a large ring nut.

The gearbox was the standard BSA heavyweight, with four speeds and footchange by a pedal on the right. The kickstarter lay behind this and, as was usual, required the gearbox to be in neutral before being used. Its mechanism lay under the outer cover with the positive stop gearchange.

The frame was a cradle type with single down, top and seat tubes and duplex rails beneath the engine. A sump plate was fitted and both engine and gearbox were held in place by large plates and suitable lugs. A head steady ran back from the rear of the engine to the frame.

Girder forks of ill repute were fitted and served as a built-in governor of performance. While it was possible to work the machine up to some 60 mph in a straight line, most riders were prudent and kept below 45 after their first bumpy corner. A single central spring provided the suspension, with fork and steering friction damper to aid handling.

The wheels were spoked and fitted with 3·25 × 19 in. tyres, normally with the universal block pattern tread. Single-sided hubs had 7 in. single leading shoe brakes and these could be hard-pressed to halt the rather heavy machine. The front wheel drove the speedometer from a drive box on the left and the instrument was mounted on the top of the forks on a bracket, which hung it out to the same side.

Above right **Taken from the M20 driver's handbook this shows the machine's controls and instruments**

Right **Italian ohv conversion for the M20 with valve springs wound to reach both valves**

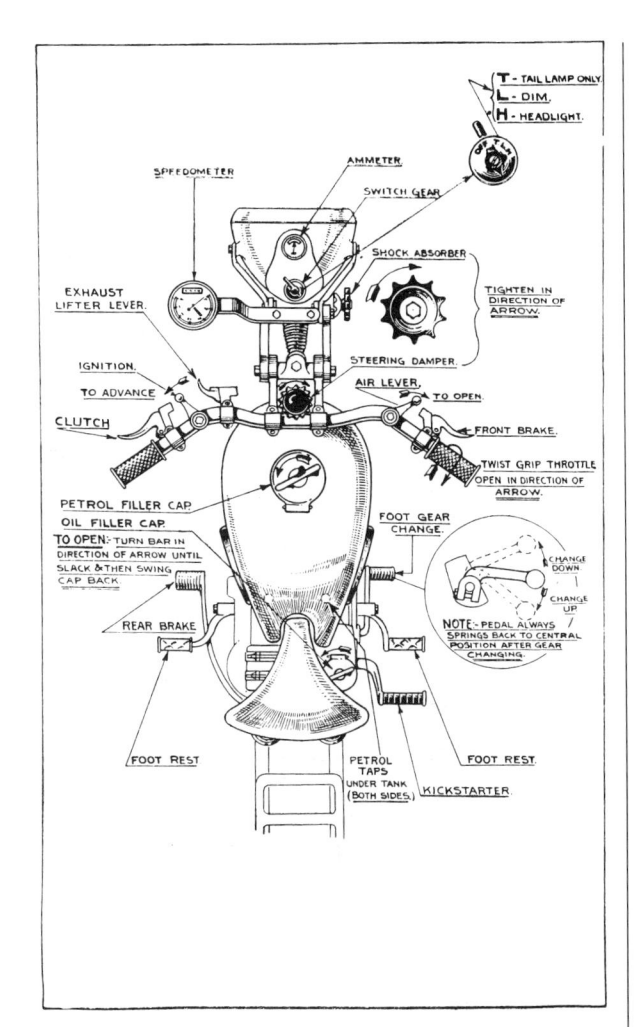

England – more makes than most

A searchlight site in Western Command where ATS officers were under training and a message delivered by M20

Small stays held the headlamp, which carried the usual blackout mask and a small panel in the rear for the ammeter and lighting switch. This last was of the four-position type with OFF, T, L and H positions.

Sturdy mudguards went round the wheels but were too close to them for serious off-road use. Under muddy conditions they would easily clog and bring machine and rider to a halt. On top of the rear one went a carrier rack to supplement the folding pannier frames, fitted on each side, which carried a canvas bag apiece. A small and uncomfortable pillion could be fitted to the carrier and rests went into lugs just ahead of the rear wheel spindle. As with the rider's footrests, no rubbers were fitted and a raised rib served to keep feet in place.

The passenger arrangement hardly seemed adequate for a poor-handling machine that could be bouncing along a rutted track. It was suggested that it was a War Office way of keeping young officers in line (only higher ranks drew a staff car) and to discourage the Don R's from giving lifts to young ladies.

The front mudguard rear stay doubled as a front stand, then common practice, and two further stands were provided. One was a massive prop that hinged from near the saddle spring mounting on the left and terminated in a sharp point with a hilt above it for support in mud. For use near GHQ, where it was tactless to dig holes

Trying the WB30 on the slopes at Bagshot. This 350 cc prototype led to the postwar B31 which was much as this model

in the general's tarmac, there was a rear stand. This took practice to use, but the art was well known to prewar riders. The trick was to hold the machine truly vertical, push the stand down with right toe, check that both sides were on the deck, move carefully to rear of machine, grasp lifting handle with both hands and give a gut-busting heave. If the machine was still upright it came up on to the stand well enough; if the rider had allowed it to sway a little he was then too far removed to catch it as it fell over.

The electric horn was attached to the top front engine plate bolt on the left side of the machine, or aft of the battery on the same side. Its button went on the handlebars, which were quite congested with levers for air, ignition and exhaust lifter as well as the usual clutch, front brake and throttle.

A toolbox was provided on the right between the chainstays and, according to the Driver's Handbook, contained a comprehensive toolkit in a bag. In all there were 20 items, including a Tecalemit grease gun, feeler gauges and a wheel alignment gauge. Additional equipment listed included tyre levers, puncture outfit, chain spares and a Wesco oil can. The last resort was a roll of insulating tape.

So BSA went to war with their side-valve plodder and of the 126,334 machines they built and supplied to the armed forces most were M20s. For all that, BSA themselves did not think too

WB30 engine unit showing the alternator strapped onto the magneto and large rocker box for the hairpin valve springs

highly of the model for army use as they considered it too heavy, rather clumsy and with insufficient ground clearance. Their ideas ran more on the lines of a machine based on something lighter and with more sporting pretensions. One such could then be amended to use their competition experience to produce a good machine for road or path use.

Early in the war they had a chance to show their ideas when the War Office asked firms for their ideas for a new machine. This was to be a 350, very light and able to cope with rough off-road conditions. BSA chose the B29 as the basis of their machine, this being the Silver Sports model that had been introduced for 1940. Although a B-range model, it used the sturdier M crankcase and so had the basis of a good strong engine. The frame and forks were B range, so the resulting model was not too heavy. Its one unusual feature lay in the cylinder head, where the overhead valves were kept under control by hairpin springs rather than the usual coils. A tool for their removal was included in the tool kit.

From this machine BSA devised the WB30, which kept much from the civilian model. The engine continued with its hairpin valve springs, the gearbox was the lighter B type and the frame the open diamond common to that range. A rather small front brake was fitted and the silencer changed from a Velocette style with fishtail to a plain cylinder, as on the M20.

The greatest change was to the electrics. Ignition remained with the faithful magneto, but strapped to its back was an alternator. This gave direct lighting for the headlamp, which also contained a dry battery for parking. A bulb horn was fitted.

Equipped with the usual panniers and headlamp mask the WB30 in normal khaki finish was much more the machine that BSA thought the services ought to use. The truth of this was to be borne out after the war when the design became the B31 and the start of a series whose competition derivatives worked very well off-road.

The War Office seemed to agree and awarded BSA a contract. Quantities of 150 and 200 have been spoken of, but the numbering ran from WB30–101 to 150, which indicates 50 machines, as all BSA numbers began at 101. The machines were built and put on test with the army, who were delighted with it; hardly surprising if their comparison standard was the M20. An order for 10,000 more WB30s was issued, but was amended to M20s as the War Office had another think, being mindful of the spares and servicing problems that could have arisen.

Any further thoughts of a lightweight 350 disappeared in the bombing of Coventry and Birmingham and the losses in the Dunkirk evacu-

Above **Line-up of police on C10 machines in 1941. The very similar ohv C11 also saw service during the war**

Below **Engine unit of the postwar BSA side-valve twin built as a prototype for military use**

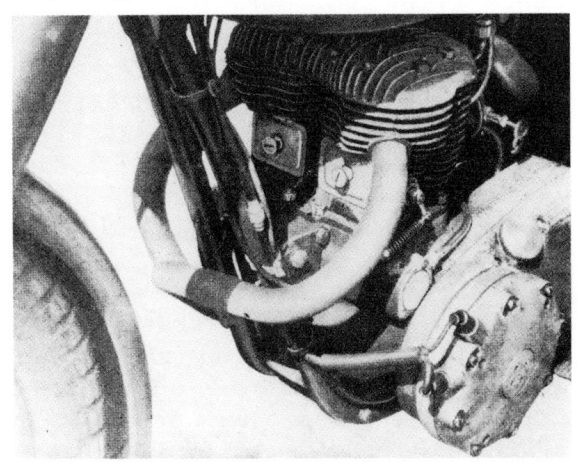

ation. After those events matters became rather grim and only production was important.

In addition to the M20, BSA also supplied 250 cc C10 models to the services. They were used for training and home station duties in the main and the machines were the simple, utilitarian model with soft side-valve engine and three-speed, footchange gearbox. They were built on the light side for the daily ride to work, so were hard pressed in service use, where they were ridden farther and faster than envisaged. In all they stood up to the thrashing well, although there were shortcomings in the dynamo regulator, gearbox fixings and rear wheels, which did not take kindly to the considerable mileage covered over rough tracks.

In addition to the C10 a batch of ohv C11s was built for service in India and these were modified in the ignition area with a mag-dyno in place of the usual coil ignition. Otherwise the model was a copy of its side-valve brother in fixtures and fittings.

At the end of the war the bulk of M20 machines that had survived were sold off, along with many of the spares; the quantities of the latter were so large that forty years later they were readily available. For the army it was a time to look into a new machine, and to meet the specification BSA produced a twin based loosely on their A7.

Like that model the two cylinders sat side by side with a gear-driven magneto tucked in behind them. The difference lay in the use of side valves, positioned in front of the one-piece cast iron block and concealed by a pair of tappet covers with a valve lifter set in their side, for use in rough country rather than to aid starting, as the compression ratio was a mere 5·8 : 1. Unlike the A7 the camshaft was set across the crankcase ahead of the crankshaft and the one-piece head was in light alloy.

An AC generator was mounted on the outside of the primary chaincase and coupled directly to the headlight. Later it was intended to add rectifier and battery to create a complete electrical system. The carburettor was a dust- and water-proof Solex tucked in behind the cylinder block with a gas passage cast into the block to connect it to the valves.

The gearbox had three speeds with foot-change and was bolted to the rear of the crankcase as usual with the early twin. The rear chain centres were also fixed, with the chain running in an all-enveloping case to the fixed rear-wheel spindle. Chain tension was set by a jockey sprocket mounted in the case itself and adjustable over an arc.

The frame was a duplex rigid cradle fitted with telescopic front forks. Drum brakes of 7 in. diameter went into the wire-spoked wheels, which were shod with 3·25 × 19 in. tyres. Straight spokes were used for both wheels. The fuel tank held 2·5 gallons and its capacity was a little reduced because the speedometer and a toolbox were both mounted in its top, the first above a tunnel and the second recessed a little. The oil tank went in its usual position on the right and the saddle could be adjusted for both height and distance back from the tank.

Full service equipment was fitted and the machine was ridden through the 1948 SSDT, where it gained an award. Despite its good showing it was not taken any further and the army kept to its M20s for many years. When it changed its BSAs it went for a military version of the B40, a 350 cc unit construction single, and for this the firm were able to exploit their competition knowledge of that series of machine.

A postwar side-effect of the many M20s left in Europe was an overhead valve conversion produced by La Mototecnica Velox of Turin. This firm made many such kits for Italian side-valve models, so the BSA one was no great challenge to them. It consisted of an alloy head and barrel, with the pushrod tunnel cast integral with each part, a piston, exhaust pipe and various detail parts.

The pushrods crossed over, as in the C11, and rose to one-piece rockers with adjusters at their outer ends. The oddest feature was the design of the valve springs, of which there were two. They were of the hairpin form but modified so that the end of each went under a collar on both inlet and exhaust valve. Thus the spring ran from one collar, went round a central cross-pin three times and then went on to the other collar. Spring two was a mirror image of spring one and the whole idea was similar to that used by a JAP 500 cc engine used by Cotton in 1939.

The result looked much like the postwar B31, except for the cylinder base studs and built-in pushrod tunnel. It was claimed to be good for 70 mph, which was a fair speed for a touring 500 running on the poor petrol of the era.

One such converted engine turned up in Australia some 35 years later, but that was just continuing the M20 theme of world-wide use.

Cotton

In 1939 Cotton introduced a model fitted with a new 500 cc ohv JAP engine designed by Dougal Marchant. It had an odd appearance for the horizontal finning of the cylinder was continued up the head, and with the pushrods in cast-in tunnels it looked like an extra tall two-stroke. The valve gear was a little unusual in that a pair of springs were used, wound in hairpin fashion but left with the ends pointing fore and aft. The wound section went on a centre pin and the ends hooked under both inlet and exhaust collars.

The same idea was used by a Turin firm after the war to produce an ohv conversion for the BSA M20 model. The JAP engine was a good puller, with a gas engine tickover and with enough power to push the Cotton along to 75 mph. It went in the famous triangulated frame that gave the make its excellent road-holding and the rigidity of this also made it suitable for sidecar work.

Thus a number were built with a box body for the local council and similar machines were sold to the Ministry of Supply for use at the oil wells

The 1939 Cotton with 500 cc JAP engine with horizontal fins and hairpin style valve springs

of the Middle East. In addition, a few of them went to the War Office, for similar carriage work, where they chugged along over a vast mileage under some hefty loads.

Douglas

The story of the Douglas motorcycle in wartime is set in the Great War of 1914–18 when many thousands of the models with flat twin engines served in Flanders and elsewhere. The stamina of the machines was quite extraordinary considering their frail construction and the conditions they had to work under. Heat, rain, cold or mud with shell holes to dodge, bullets and often a continuous bombardment made dispatch riding a hazardous job, but the machines were quite reliable and even the tyres seemed to stand the strain well.

The Douglas was prone to the front plug shorting in the wet and the forks were likely to succumb to the thrashing they received, this being a problem common to all the models used on the Western Front. To avoid a serious crash the riders bound the forks so that if, or rather when, the spring broke the forks did not collapse. The other universal precaution was a large box bolted to the rear carrier into which went spares to cover most contingencies.

When World War 2 broke out the Douglas firm was in the throes of one of its periodic problem times. Motorcycle production was virtually at a standstill and much of the equipment used in its manufacture had been sold off. Thus, while the firm was very active throughout the war years, it was engaged mainly on work for the Ministry of Aircraft Production. Industrial trucks continued to be built and the firm also made all types of stationary engines, so did not lose touch with the internal combustion engine over this period.

On the issue of the new machine specification from the Ministry of Supply, Douglas decided to build a suitable machine using both their wartime experience and postwar plans. The outcome was the DV60 prototype, with horizontally opposed flat twin engine.

The engine dimensions were 74 × 70 mm, which gave a capacity of 602 cc. The compression ratio was 6·25:1, fairly high for an engine with side valves. Thanks to the combination of this feature and the short stroke the engine was

The Douglas DV60 built just after the war with leading link forks and fully enclosed rear chain

commendably narrow. The heads and barrels were both in light alloy and the latter were fitted with iron liners. The valves were positioned above the cylinders and the tappets were therefore easily accessible under a plate held by a single thumb screw.

The valves were opened by a single camshaft positioned above the crank, which was fitted into a one-piece crankcase. On top of this went the magneto to supply the sparks and on the crankshaft nose went an alternator to power the lights. It was intended to add a rectifier at a later stage.

A single-plate clutch connected the drive to a three-speed gearbox bolted to the rear of the engine. Both footchange pedal and kickstart lever went on the right and the gearbox contained a bevel gear pair to turn the drive for the chain, which connected to the rear wheel. This chain was fully enclosed in a light alloy oil bath case with separate tunnels for top and bottom runs. Flexible bellows at the forward ends joined the case to the gearbox sprocket housing and provided the variation in length needed to accommodate chain adjustment and the needed wheel movement.

The carburettor was a single Solex with cold-start device and supplied both cylinders. It bolted to a face at the rear of the crankcase and an integral manifold carried the mixture to a pipe on each side which completed the job and connected to the cylinder. An air filter fed the car-

Right side of DV60 showing saddle suspension and protected fuel tank

burettor. Both exhaust pipes curled down under the engine and connected to a single silencer box.

The frame that carried this unit was of duplex form, welded construction and rigid. The top tubes ran straight from headstock to rear wheel spindle, while the down tubes curled under the engine to run back to the same point but with one further bend in them. Tubes also ran horizontally from the down tubes to the seat pillar point and the fuel tank went into the resulting triangle, which gave it a measure of protection even if it did nothing for the appearance. This was further distorted by the saddle and its mounting. The seat itself was a normal frame and cover but was not mounted on the usual springs. Instead it sat on a massive telescopic seat pillar, which allowed it to move vertically over some three inches of travel. A bracket ran forward to the frame to brace the mounting and prevent the seat, and rider, from spinning like a top.

The front forks were Douglas Radiadraulic with leading links and hydraulic damping. Both wheels were quickly detachable and were built up using straight spokes, which called for special hubs. Both brakes were of 8 in. diameter and the rim size was 19 in. The front tyre was of 3·25 in. section, but the rear was subject to discussion and provision was made in terms of mudguard and frame clearance to allow up to 5 in. section.

The front mudguard was sprung and had a massive valance to partly fill up the gap between it and the tyre. It was supported by long stays anchored at the fork ends and to the lower fork crown. The rear mudguard was conventional and surmounted by a hefty rear carrier, which bolted directly to the frame. On it could be hung pannier frames and bags while a pillion pad could go on top. The pillion rests were unusual for they comprised a vertical rod on which the rest pivoted to point forward when not needed and out when in use.

In all a machine of strange looks and strictly functional. But not functional enough, it seemed, for the one that ran in the 1948 Scottish had to retire and in all just three prototypes were built.

James

The Greet factory only produced one model for the services during the war as much of their effort was concentrated on shells, aircraft fittings and other armament parts. Furthermore their efforts were hampered by the blitz, much of their plant being badly damaged in 1940.

It was quickly rebuilt and in 1943 their Military Lightweight or ML model went into production. The machine was a lightweight and built for use by paratroops, so it had to be able to withstand parachute landings. Its purpose was to aid the rapid dispersal, concentration or movement of men once they were on the ground and this was to prove an excellent idea and use.

The machines were light enough to be carried over obstacles if necessary so were ideal for troops that might need to land and move a few miles in a hurry and to shoot straight, for they got there faster and without arriving out of breath. They were also cheap enough to abandon, suitably damaged, if no recovery looked possible, and able to carry a fair load when called upon to do so.

The ML was based on a prewar lightweight and was fitted with a Villiers 9D engine of 122 cc. This had dimensions of 50 × 62 mm and was of unit construction with the three-speed gearbox built in one with the engine. The castings were split vertically and the construction was typical Villiers with bob-weights, pressed-up flywheels, bronze and steel uncaged rollers for the big end, cast iron barrel on studs and light alloy cylinder head with decompressor in one side and sparking plug in the other.

Twin exhaust ports were used, with a cast manifold bolted on to each side of the cylinder, which had four transfer ports. These were disposed to front and rear, while the single inlet was

Left **Villiers 9D engine unit with three-speed hand change gearbox as used in the James**

Below **James advertisement for the Clockwork Mouse as the 125 was known. Postwar it ran on as the ML and then the Cadet model series**

THE FAMOUS JAMES *"Go anywhere Lightweight"*

These James Motor Cycles are being used by our Airborne Forces for the toughest, roughest work a motor cycle can be put to. That in itself speaks volumes for the post-war James models, which will be a delight to ride and provide the world's most economical motoring.

THE JAMES 125 c.c. MILITARY LIGHTWEIGHT

AS USED BY OUR AIRBORNE FORCES

England – more makes than most

61

The James Military Lightweight which proved so handy and easy to use under combat conditions

below the exhaust on the left. From the port a curved light alloy manifold ran round to the back of the barrel and the Villiers carburettor. To this was attached an intake pipe in which was fitted a butterfly choke with two-position lever on the left. At the outer end went an oil-wetted air filter of cylindrical form.

The two exhaust manifolds were connected by short curved pipes to a cylindrical silencer body set across the machine ahead of the engine. From it a single pipe ran back on the left to a second silencer and a tailpipe.

Ignition was by flywheel magneto mounted on the right end of the crankshaft with an external rotor, which ran without any cover. Behind it went the stator bolted to the crankcase, and this carried lighting coils in addition to the ignition one. The lights, just a headlamp with mask and a tail light, were thus dependant on the engine running and were controlled by a switch in the back of the headlamp.

The primary drive by single-strand chain went in a light alloy case on the left and drove a very conventional three-speed gearbox. Gear selection was by hand with a rather slack mechanism between the selector fork and the outer lever. This in turn was connected by a rod to the change lever mounted with its gate to the right of the petrol tank. Final drive was by chain on the left.

The engine unit went into a rigid frame with bolted-on rear tubes and simple blade girder forks. Suspension was by a single central barrel spring and no damping was provided, the system having to rely on the friction in the spindles and bushes. Wheels were wire spoked with minute drum brakes of the single leading shoe pattern and were shod with 2·75 × 19 in. tyres on WM0 rims. Equipment comprised simple-blade mudguards, a saddle, a fuel tank and a centre stand.

The machine was known as the clockwork mouse and nearly 6000 of them were built in the war. After it the model served well in the James range until 1948, and in that time another 20,000 were made, only altered in detail and finish.

Norton

When the war broke out Norton were hard at work on military contracts that had been issued earlier as a result of Gilbert Smith's badgering of the War Office.

The machine they were building in some number was the side-valve 16H model, frozen in its 1937 form with a few minor changes to make it more suited to service use. For this it was a most useful machine, being simple, easy to service and cheap enough to abandon when all else failed.

Most of all it had the merit of reliability and a lineage stretching back many years with little change. The side-valve engine dated back to the earliest days of the company, when it was a single-gear model with belt drive, while the 1937 machine was in truth little altered from its near-vintage forebear of 1931.

It was that year when Norton made one of their few real changes to their models and adopted dry sump lubrication, moved the magneto behind the cylinder and updated the frame. As the 1930s progressed the transmission changed to the Norton clutch, gearbox and chaincase, the forks gained check springs, the dynamo a regulator and there were minor detail improvements.

In 1938 the valve gear was enclosed, but the War Office held off from that, as yet untried, innovation when ordering and settled for the 1937 arrangement of a pressed steel cover and grease nipples for the valve guides.

The engine was as basic and traditional as only a side-valve Norton could be. Dimensions were the famous 79 × 100 mm and the capacity 490 cc. Construction was simple and standard English, with the head and barrel in cast iron, built-up flywheels in vertically split crankcase and chain-driven mag-dyno. An Amal type six provided the mixture and the exhaust ran low down along the right side, where it had been since 1932.

The gearbox was the four-speed one developed from the Sturmey Archer design when that went out of production, and its footchange had an external linkage to the camplate. Maladjustment or wear led to missed gears, but always one could be found to keep the machine going. The clutch that drove the box came from the same background and its ability to separate its plates well was part of the key to the good Norton gearchange.

To house these well-proven units Norton chose their existing trials frame, which gave them a little more ground clearance. It was still an open diamond type with rigid rear end, to which was bolted a typical rear stand of the era. With the frame came a crankcase shield. The forks were the trials girder type with built-in buffer stops, one on each side. In other respects it was the standard Norton fork, with check springs and dampers for both the fork action and the steering.

The rest of the machine was built up using mostly standard parts. The wheels had the brake drums held to the hubs by three long studs, prone to coming loose at the rear, and were of normal wire spoke construction. The brakes were single leading shoe with a separate pivot pin for each shoe. Mudguards were steel with the rear stay of the front one doubling as a front stand.

The oil tank was small and rectangular with wing nut filler cap, and the petrol tank lacked the instrument panel of the civilian machine. The toolbox was either the stock item bolted to the chinstays on the right or a new part mounted alongside the rear carrier, although still on the right. The peacetime lock went and was replaced by a knurled knob or a one-armed wing screw. The theory of the latter was that it might loosen but the offset weight would not allow it to undo under vibration.

A saddle was used and a pillion pad could be added to the rear carrier. The rearmost of the stays that took any passenger weight was extended out so that it could also act as a lifting

England – more makes than most

63

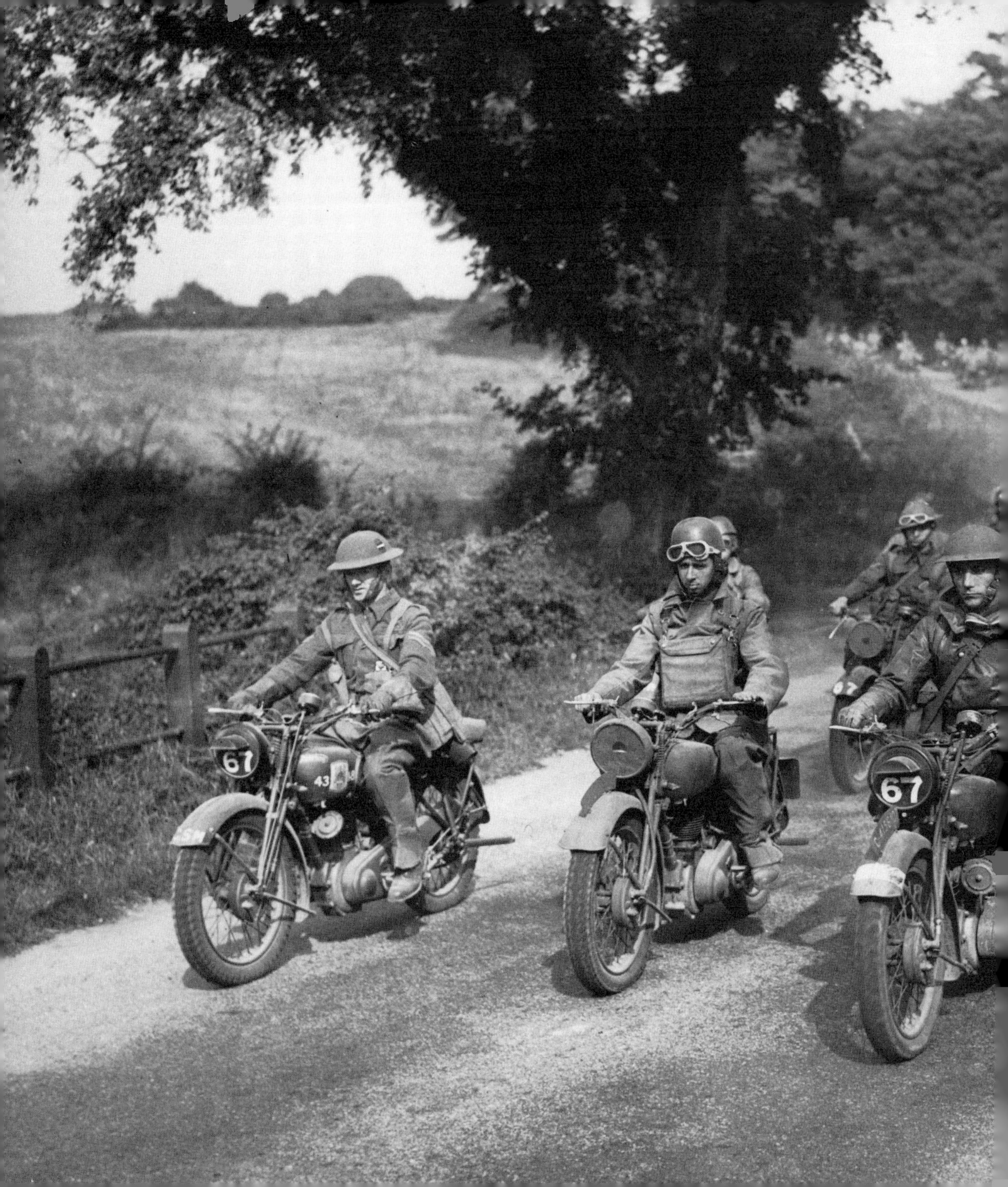
67
43
67

Above **Not many were able to commandeer an International for dispatch rider duties**

Left **Norton riders 'on exercises' as the saying went during 1941. Few wear goggles despite the dry conditions**

handle when using the rear stand. The horn hung from a lug on the front down tube and the big 8 in. headlamp was supported on a pair of prongs in standard Norton style. The lighting switch and an ammeter went in a small panel set in the rear of the lamp shell.

The speedometer went on top of the forks in the centre, where it was driven from a gearbox fixed to the front brake backplate. The battery went on the left, opposite the oil tank, and the dynamo regulator was fixed on top of the upper right chainstay. The small details were stock, so the gear pedal kept its rubber and indicator pointer, while the footrests were traditional with their small end plates and shaped rubbers.

In time the economies of war changed them to trial-type tubes with a disc at the end to stop the rider's boot from sliding off. Handlebar grips became webbing, the headlamp was reduced in size and the speedometer moved on to a bracket on the left to stop its cable being trapped in the forks.

That aside the 16H was just built, and built to the tune of around 100,000 machines. The faults that the riders soon came to terms with were

65

The 16H Norton as built in large numbers except that this one has the telescopic front forks that postwar become Roadholders

Not easy with a 16H but the combination of a sharp rise and a Canadian rider produced this shot

the slop in the gear change linkage, the ignition area floating about or the rear wheel nuts falling off. All could be dealt with in the field if the alternative was walking, so the bikes kept going.

More of a workshop problem was the gearbox mounting, which suffered if allowed to work loose. The frame would then chew into the forked lug and increase the clearance. When tightened, one or both lugs could snap off, but the machine was still usable.

There were variants from the standard issue for use overseas and in the desert. For this work it was fitted with a massive air filter mounted to the right above the pillion footrest and connected by hose to the carburettor. Colours varied according to the service for which they were built and most were rebuilt at least once during their service life, when they would lose their original identity and often emerge from workshops in a totally new shade of paint.

As soon as Norton had a contract for 16H machines Gilbert Smith began to pester the ministry for another to develop and build a sidecar outfit for the motorized cavalry. He succeeded in this and again they were able to draw on a standard model and couple it to their competition experience. In prewar days Dennis

Mansell, son of the Norton managing director at that time, had campaigned an outfit with sidecar wheel drive in trials whenever allowed. Thanks to this the firm had a good idea of the problems involved and their solution.

The base machine they started from was the Big 4, with its 82 × 120 mm dimensions and 634 cc capacity. Like the 16H it ran on a very modest compression ratio for its side-valve engine and had hefty flywheels. The combination gave it tree-stump pulling power coupled with all the usual Norton features.

The engine used was the 1938 type, with fully enclosed valves, and much of the machine was as the 16H. The main change was the addition of the sidecar, based on a standard Norton chassis, and the modifications needed to drive both rear wheels. The result of the work gave a live rear wheel spindle from which the sidecar drive was taken by a shaft running across the chassis to its wheel. A simple dog clutch was incorporated in this drive and controlled by a hand lever to engage it when required.

To accommodate this mechanism the rear fork ends of the frame were enlarged to carry bearings for the spindle. In the process the frame and forks were also modified to accommodate

A 16H of the RAF being ridden through Lille by a Belgian pilot in 1944 en route to see his parents after four years out of touch. Note spare petrol can

67

The tank top air cleaner as fitted to the 16H with crude carburettor connection

a 4 in. knobbly trials-type tyre and give it some clearance.

The sidecar was based on the standard Norton chassis, which had the wheel supported on both sides with a through spindle. This not only avoided the strains of a stub axle but also the outer chassis tube gave the wheel a degree of protection and firm support for its mudguard.

The chassis was altered to a live wheel spindle with bearings fixed into the chassis lugs. The sidecar wheel was the same three-bolt type as the others, so all were interchangeable, with a spare carried on the back of the sparse sidecar body. This was of the simplest with a seat, stowage box at the rear and a front section on the lines of a trials chair. Grab handles were provided front and rear, while the body front panel was large enough to offer some protection to the occupant. Entry and exit were easy – suitable even when a dive into a ditch was the best manoeuvre.

There were further handles at front and rear to help if the machine was stuck. At the rear a pair of tubes ran back from the saddle nose to the rear mudguard, where they joined to form a handle. They were held in place by vertical tubes, of chainstay proportions, which ran down to the wheel spindle and bore the passenger's weight.

At the front went an extra wide mudguard with a lifting handle, which doubled as a front stay. The mudguard was wider than the forks and to accommodate them was pierced around mid-point for the fork blades to pass through with a supporting plate for bracing. It was also normal practice to fit large mudguard valances, which enclosed the sides in from the guard to the wheel centre.

The outfits were used in this basic form and in others. The usual fitment was a machine gun on a swivel mount, but other weapons could be accommodated. One such was a mortar, and in this case the sidecar body was changed for a platform carrying the firing tube on its tripod legs and two boxes of ammunition.

Once the Big 4 went on test it soon became clear that it was not really up to the job of pulling all the weight through mud on knobbly tyres. The traction was there but not the power to make it work. So the engine was tuned in classic side-valve fashion by moving the combustion chamber volume so it was no longer as the 1938 motor. This did not matter to the army, who only had to stock the new items and 16H pieces.

Several thousand sidecar outfits were built and used mainly for reconnaissance work in the early years, with many going to North Africa. This experience suggested improvements, and so a second version was put in hand in prototype form by the War Office. Although the sidecar remained as the Big 4 the machine was built by AMC with an ohv Matchless engine of 1000 cc in a move to give the outfit the power and grunt it needed to cope with heavy going. At the same time a car-type rear axle was proposed to enclose the exposed mechanism, which suffered undue wear and tear in its original form. It was also given a reverse gear to enable the driver to back out of tricky situations and dead ends and

Batch of Nortons in the sheds at Southampton docks prior to being shipped to Palestine in 1936

is described under AMC.

Then came Lease-Lend and with it the Jeep, which went most places, carried more, could be driven by anyone and was a shield to hide under in times of stress. While a really skilfully driven chair could get through situations that would stop a Jeep, such skill was hard to come by in an army. In average hands they could be a mobile disaster, not helped by the lack of sidecar wheel lead dictated by the design. So the War Office blessed the Jeep and dumped its sidecars.

Some of them did reach the civilian market after the war but with the sidecar drive flame cut away to ensure no comeback from accident claims. The army knew only too well that if you forgot to disengage the sidecar drive when you left the rough and returned to tarmac you were in trouble. With heavy tyres and no differential it just went straight on at the first corner even if put on full lock.

There was one other wartime Norton and this came into being in response to the War Office specification for a very light 350. To get the weight down Norton built an all-alloy side-valve engine and put it in a welded frame with light but non-detachable wheels. Various details were in light alloy, including the handlebars and levers, and the firm were given a contract to build 50 machines for test on active service.

Nearly all went to France and were abandoned in the retreat to Dunkirk, after which matters were grim. Interesting experiments had to be forgotten and 16Hs built as fast as possible. Not until much later was there time to stop and think, and one result was a 16H with telescopic front forks. These were developed from the pre-war ones used by the works racers to add hydraulic damping; postwar they became the Roadholders.

They, of course, were not for the Don R, but for all that the girder 16H handled in the taut manner of a Norton until the bushes wore. In other respects it was more suited than some for its work for it was quick enough, had adequate brakes, better ground clearance than most and could work its way along tracks, past a convoy or through mud as required.

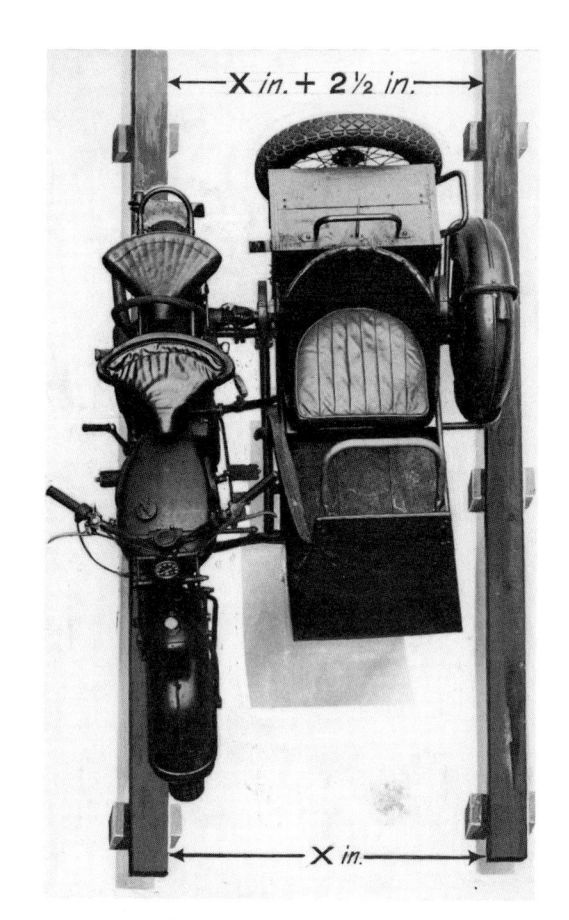

Small wonder it was built in such large numbers and accounted for close to a quarter of British wartime production.

After the war Norton got on with the building of their civilian road models and their famous Manx. Later came their Dominator twin, and it was this engine that was used as the basis of a one-off military machine to oppose the Triumph TRW.

The Norton twin used the standard bottom half, and its front-mounted camshaft was ideally placed for the side-valve barrel clamped to it. It went into a rigid frame with a set of standard cycle parts finished in drab olive green and thus made an instant machine. It failed to impress the War Office, however, and no more was heard of it.

Left **Big 4 and sidecar showing the measurement of toe-in**

Below **Big 4 rear view showing the sidecar wheel drive and dog clutch to connect it to the rear wheel**

Part of a batch of seven 16H machines being packed into a crate for shipment from the works. Note pannier frames on crate base

Royal Enfield

With their slogan 'built like a gun' Royal Enfield machines had to be a natural for the services in wartime. The firm was Victorian in its origins and had built their first powered machine, a quad, back in 1898. Thus they were well established when World War 1 broke out, but during this were kept nearly totally on munitions production. They did produce a small number of special sidecar outfits constructed either to mount a machine gun or to carry the wounded. A case of cause and effect, one might say.

After that they experienced the ups and downs of the industry over the following two decades, and in the 1930s concentrated on simple singles that people actually got their money out for. This kept the firm in good order, so it was no surprise that in World War 2 they became a major motorcycle supplier. They also made a great deal of other equipment, including stationary engines and armaments.

Their smallest machine they owed to the Germans. In prewar days the 98 cc DKW model RT was sold in Holland by a firm owned by Jews, so in 1938 the concession was cancelled overnight and went elsewhere. Determined not to be beaten, the firm took an RT98 to England and finished up at Enfields, who they asked to make a copy but of 125 cc. The outcome was just that, a ringer, except for the capacity increase, down to the flying wing transfer on the tank. The model was to be called the Royal Baby, so its initials would be similar.

A few machines were delivered in 1939, but with the outbreak of war this ceased and the tooling went into store at Redditch. In 1942 the notion of using a really light motorcycle in the front line and for dropping with airborne troops was taken up by the army. The Enfield was a natural for this work and being all tooled up and developed it was easy to put it into production. With airborne use it soon gained its nickname – the 'Flying Flea'.

The Flea engine was of unit construction with a vertically split crankcase containing the three-speed gearbox as well as the crankshaft. Dimensions were 54 × 55 mm, so the capacity was 126 cc. The crankshaft ran in three ball races and an outrigger bearing, while crankcase sealing was achieved with reamered bronze bushes on each side. A bob-weight crank was used with an uncaged big end. The barrel was cast in iron and the head in light alloy, with plug to one side and decompressor to the other.

A flywheel magneto went on the right to provide ignition and lighting, with the points cam on the extreme end of the crankshaft. A single-strand chain on the left took the drive to the single-plate clutch and was enclosed by a steel case. The gearbox ratios were selected by a hand lever working in a gate bolted to the right side of the tank. The kickstarter pedal folded away and the exhaust and silencer went on the right. On many machines two silencers were used, the first a cylindrical one set across in front of the crankcase and the second the normal tubular one on the right. Engine lubrication was by petroil.

The engine unit went into a simple tubular rigid frame fitted with blade girder forks controlled by rubber bands. The wheels had wire spokes, small drum brakes and skimpy mudguards. Equipment comprised a saddle, rear carrier, cylindrical toolbox, which went under the saddle, and lights. The headlight was either of the usual size fitted with a mask or a much smaller cycle type.

The whole machine could be fitted into a tubular crate to which was attached its parachute. To aid packing the bars could be turned easily as they were held by a bicycle-type stem bolt with a built-in wing nut. The fuel tank cap had a screw-down vent so it was only a moment's work to release the machine on the ground and bring it into action. Thanks to its light weight it could be man-handled over obstacles and gave the troops mobility.

The Flea also went into action in gliders, was carried on tanks to act as a tender, when needed, and served well on beach-heads to direct men and materials. After the war it was demobbed, painted black and continued in production in various forms up to 1962.

The bulk of the remaining World War 2 Royal Enfields were of 346 cc and based on prewar models. Two versions were built, the side-valve

ATS dispatch riders running to their Royal Enfields. These are 250 cc D/D models used for training and the time is April 1941

model C and the overhead valve model CO, but aside from the head and barrel they were the same.

In typical Enfield fashion the vertically split crankcase included the oil tank for the dry sump system. Within this was the crankcase wall itself and in that turned the built-up flywheels with plain bush big end. A train of gears on the right in the timing chest turned the cams and drove the mag-dyno, while the oil pumps and filter went below the crankshaft gear.

Head and barrel were in cast iron and the valve gear was fully enclosed on both models. On the ohv engine the one-piece rockers were held in split clamps, which assembled on studs under a light alloy lid. A plate in the side of the barrel gave access to the tappet adjusters at the lower ends of the pushrods and below these went flat-faced tappets. A similar plate on the side-valve engine did the same job.

The gearbox was separately mounted in plates and chain driven from the engine. On all the C models and most of the COs an Albion box was fitted, but on contract 294/C/19870 Burman units were used. In either case they had four speeds

August 1940 and a Royal Enfield model C takes part in manoeuvres in the Midlands in a combined army and police exercise

and a footchange on the right, but the Burman lacked the cush drive centre of the Albion.

The Lucas electrics included a regulator under the saddle, a battery on the left, a headlamp with ammeter and switch mounted in a panel attached to the shell and a horn bolted to the front engine fixing. The carburettor was the usual Amal type six with separate float chamber and the exhaust went on the right.

The frame was rigid, with twin tubes beneath the engine and gearbox that gave good protection to the rather large crankcase casting. Front forks were girders with single central barrel spring and dampers for both fork movement and steering. Wheels were wire spoked with drum brakes, the front one driving the fork-mounted speedometer from a drive box screwed into the back of the brake plate.

Equipment was to the normal service standard with saddle, rear carrier, masked lights and a hefty prop stand with a spike for use on muddy ground. The propstand pivoted in the left rear wheel spindle plate so was really too far to the rear to function well. The model C also had a centre stand and the CO both front and rear stands, the first doubling as a mudguard stay.

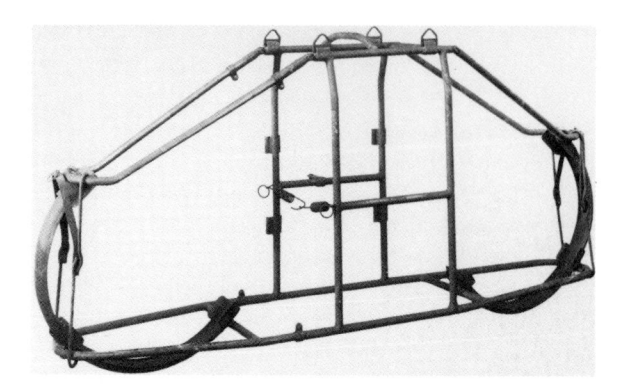

The Flying Flea birdcage used to drop the model by parachute

In addition to the two 350s Enfield also built a batch of side-valve 570s for the navy and about 1000 of the 250 cc side-valve model D/D for training use. Both followed the lines of the model C, although the 250 was generally lighter in construction as befitted its more mundane performance. A few 350 cc model G and 500 cc model J machines were also built, possibly to utilize some spares stock.

The remaining wartime Enfields were prototypes plus a few CO models fitted with telescopic

Enfield toolboxes as packed to please on parade

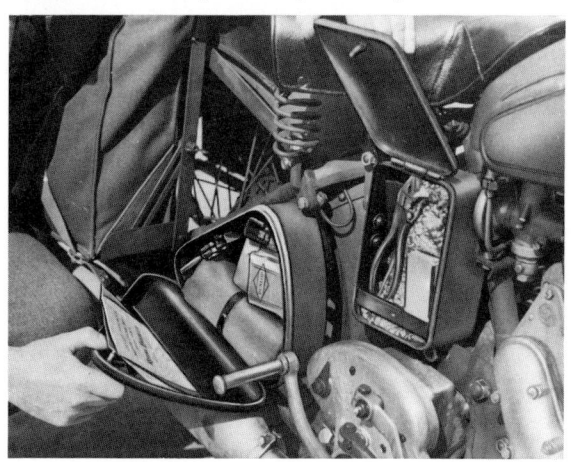

Two Fleas tied down in a Horsa glider for a training drop in April 1944. A few weeks later it was the real thing over Normandy

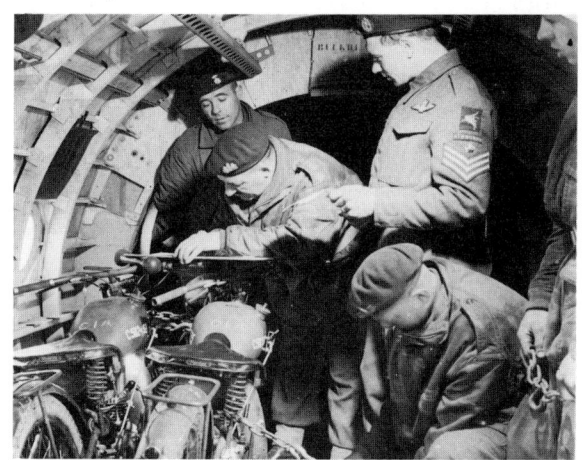

Fleas in use with paratroops who also rode folding bicycles if need be

front forks and a deeply valanced front mudguard. These appeared as early as 1941, the Redditch firm having no difficulty keeping up with the trends that mattered. Of the prototypes one was a lightweight side-valve 350 built to meet the early War Office specification and forgotten with all the others after the Coventry bombing.

The other prototype came in response to the later specification and was a 350 cc side-valve twin. Its appearance was a little unusual for the two parallel cylinders cast in one iron block were laid back a little, although their fins remained parallel to the ground. The head joint was, however, angled back with the head to match. Carburettor, exhaust pipes and valves were all at the front and the pipes joined on the right to connect to a single silencer.

An Albion gearbox with footchange was used, with both drive chains enclosed in one vast chaincase, in which a jockey sprocket tensioned the rear chain. The oil tank was not built into the crankcase and the lubrication system was dry sump. Ignition was by magneto with a dynamo strapped to its back and the lighting was simple.

The frame was rigid with girder front forks, and at the rear the seat and most of the mudguard could be removed by releasing a few nuts. The rear tyre was a fat 4·50 × 17 in.

The twin was an interesting exercise, but only

the one was built and the same fate awaited another and bigger twin. This had its cylinders in vee formation and was built as a sidecar outfit with drive to the sidecar wheel in the manner of the Big 4 Norton and the German BMW and Zundapp models.

In the main Royal Enfield just concentrated on building the two 350s and the 125 Flea. At the end of the war they continued with the CO as the G, and the Flea as the RE, while many wartime machines were refurbished and sold to a transport-hungry public. Enfields themselves joined in this exercise with black and gold C and CO models included in their catalogue, still with their girder forks. After a year or so they just concentrated on their newer G and J models, but the stream of dealer-prepared ex-War Department models continued for a good few years.

Triumph

At the outbreak of war the authorities descended on the Triumph Coventry works and took the entire stock of machines. Thus a few lucky riders drew new Speed Twins and Tiger 100s for their service work, although the less fortunate did find themselves aboard a more sober 2H or 3S.

In truth the twins could be a little too much once well run-in, for the Triumph girder forks were less than good when worn, while a nicely loosened Tiger engine was fast. Worn to the point of needing attention, even more power would be on tap, the oil would seep from the seams and progress became really exciting as the bike twitched and weaved at speed.

Thus the authorities settled for an order for the 350 cc side-valve model 3SW as being more suited to their needs and personnel. This was based on the civilian 3S and was typical of Triumph singles of the late 1930s. The whole series had been designed by Val Page in 1932 much on the lines of his older Ariel single and in a layout he repeated at BSA in 1937.

By then Edward Turner was running Triumph and adding his styling touches to the range that rang the bell with the buying public. Backing the sporting Tiger models were the standard ohv ones and for the prosaic market the side-valve series, with the 350 at the bottom of the list. Just the job for the services thought the authorities, although Turner was to prefer twins.

The model 3SW was very English in its construction. The engine shared its bottom half with the 500 so was a long-stroke when built as a 350, at dimensions of 70 × 89 mm. The crankshaft was built up with heavy flywheels fitted with mainshafts secured on a keyed taper by a large unit. The big end was a double row of rollers running uncaged on a crankpin pulled up on tapers by nuts. The connecting rod was sleeved for the rollers and bushed for the gudgeon pin.

The piston ran in an iron barrel with the valve chest cast into the side, fully enclosing the valve gear. Each valve was opened by its own cam and tappet, and each camshaft was gear driven from the crankshaft. The gear train was extended to the rear of the engine to drive a mag-dyno, which provided ignition and electric power.

The crankcase was split vertically on its centre line and a single cover enclosed the timing gears. The double plunger oil pump was bolted on to it and driven from the exhaust camshaft with a further small round cover. The lubrication system was dry sump, with the oil tank beneath the saddle on the right being balanced by the battery on the left. Between them went the voltage regulator.

The transmission was by chain and a cam lobe shock absorber went on the left crankshaft end. The primary chain and clutch were enclosed in a smart light alloy case and drove a four-speed gearbox with footchange. This was the standard Triumph unit and of conventional English design.

The frame was a bolted-up cradle with single top and down tubes but twin rails running under the engine and back to the rear wheel. The front

1940 picture taken after Dunkirk with a side-valve Triumph that got back with the men

forks were girders with single barrel compression spring and steering and suspension friction dampers. They supported the headlight, with its mask and small panel with ammeter and switch, the front wheel driven speedometer and rigidly clamped handlebars. The normal Triumph rubber mounting was dispensed with as it could move under arduous conditions, it was more expensive, rubber was in short supply and who cared about isolating service riders from vibration.

The remainder of the machine was essentially stock, with the usual military additions of panniers and lifting handles, drab finish and no plat-

ing. It was not a very exciting machine.

Early in 1940 the 3SW was joined by its larger brother, the 5SW. This was ordered by the French and the extra capacity came from an 84 mm bore, which, with the common 89 mm stroke, gave 493 cc. In most other respects it was a copy of the 350 with the gearing raised by two teeth on both engine and gearbox sprockets.

In the early days of the war Triumph were working hard on their prototype to meet the Ministry specification for a single service ma-

Triumph single in 1943 in use with the ATS in Northern Ireland

chine. Edward Turner cut the development time for his model by modifying the Tiger 85, which had been cut short when the war started. This was a sports 350 cc twin intended to replace the single cylinder Tiger 80 in the same way that the Tiger 100 has taken over from the Tiger 90.

The new twin was so near to production that the magazines already had the announcement and description ready for printing. At the very last moment this pre-season feature had to be pulled out, although one magazine cover carried a headline of the new British twin. With this start it was easy enough to modify the machine and produce a prototype, which was typed the 3TW.

The parallel twin-cylinder engine had many features that were to be continued postwar in a similar civilian machine. The general layout was as for the prewar twins with one-piece block, vertically split light alloy crankcase, camshafts fore and aft of the crankshaft and gear drive to the camshafts and magneto. Different were the head cast in one with the rocker boxes and the crankshaft. This was built up from two overhung cranks, which were clamped into a central flywheel that allowed the use of plain big end bearings. Unlike the 500 both head and barrel were held down by through-bolts and a single downdraught carburettor was fitted. The exhaust pipes joined into one on the left and this continued above the chaincase to a single silencer.

The early engine was an all-alloy unit to keep the weight low, but later ones used iron as alloy supplies dwindled. Ignition was by magneto, but the direct lighting was powered by a small alternator set in the timing chest. Later models had this transferred to the primary chaincase and driven from the left crankshaft end.

The gearbox contained three speeds and was bolted to the rear of the crankcase. It was driven by a duplex chain tensioned by a slipper beneath the lower run and both pedals went on the right. The final drive went on the left under a guard. The frame was of the cradle type with rigid rear and girder forks at the front. Unusual was the petrol tank, which was designed as a bolted-in frame member running from the headstock to the saddle nose. Internally it had a channel section member to take the loads and the outer skin was a single pressing on each side, seam welded round the middle, which was easier to construct and gave more capacity.

The rest of the machine was straightforward, with drum brakes, a saddle, oil tank on the right, air cleaner beside it, toolbox beneath it and small rear carrier. In its original all-alloy form it scaled 230 lb and with an iron engine was no more than 263 lb. Even the footrests were in light alloy at first.

The first model was a flier, for the power was all above 3000 rpm and the light weight made it fast and fun to ride. Really too fast and far too

The official 400,000th British WD machine, a 350 ohv Triumph, with Edward Turner standing on the left. Makers drew lots to determine whose machine it would be

much fun for the War Office to approve for the services, so a heavier flywheel and smaller carburettor were fitted. This made all the difference and the Triumph twin was selected as the machine for the armed forces.

With this success in the palm of their hand Triumph had reason to smile, for the idea was that all firms would build the one model. Then came the Coventry bombing in November 1940 and the plans and the factory were laid to waste. The firm salvaged what they could and worked from temporary quarters in Warwick until they re-established themselves at Meridan in a new factory, but it was 1942 before that site was in operation.

From 1941 onwards the firm built 350 cc machines for the services, some the 3SW and many more its overhead-valve variant the 3HW. Like the side-valve model this was based on the prewar range and in many areas it used common parts. It took one idea from the 350 cc twin in that the head and rocker box was cast in iron in one and thanks to this the appearance of the top end of the engine differed from the civilian 3H. In place of the rocker support plates there were two pushrod tubes running up to the head and a round access cover on the side of the rocker box.

Otherwise the ohv machine followed the lines

The 350 cc 3TW Triumph which was to have been the armed forces' motorcycle until Coventry was bombed

of the side-valve models. The gearing was up one tooth on the engine from the 350 cc side valve, but for the rest it was the same. As with the Royal Enfield it was hard to see the merit of having two such similar machines in use as the extra power of the ohv engine was hardly likely to make that much difference.

However, the 3HW was a good performer and went mainly to the navy, who liked it, while the

Below left **Engine unit of the 3HW single with integral rocker box and round access cover**

Below **3TW engine on which the postwar 350 twin was based. Two into one exhaust, air filter under saddle**

3SW was used a great deal by the WRNS. In this way the spares problem was lessened as the one service could easily cope with both models.

Triumph did not give up the idea of a military twin after the Coventry blitz but went on to build the 5TW, a 500 cc side-valve twin designed by Bert Hopwood. This used the crankshaft, rods and flywheel from the Speed Twin but with side valves set in line across the front of the cast iron block. They were lifted by a single camshaft and a set of tappets with adjusters in them and the valves were restrained by dual springs.

The camshafts and crankshaft both ran in a typical Triumph twin-style crankcase just modified to leave out the rear inlet camshaft. What was different was the camshaft drive, which was by chain from the crankshaft with a rear-mounted dynamo included in the train. A slipper kept the chain in tension and the dynamo, which ran at engine speed, incorporated points and auto-advance for the coil ignition system used. On the end of the camshaft went a nut with an offset pin that drove a twin-plunger oil pump mounted in the timing chest to provide a dry sump system. The whole of the timing chest layout was just as that of the Ariel Square Four. A triangular cover enclosed the works.

The valve gear was enclosed by a pair of tappet covers and the exhaust ports splayed out a little from the corners of the block. They were threaded to take the screwed rings that retained the pipes and these led to low-level silencers on each side of the machine.

The inlet side was a little more tricky as the carburettor sat behind the block, so the inlet

A row of called up Tiger 100 machines finished for the forces but retaining the 1939 megaphone silencer

The 5TW with 500 cc side-valve twin engine and the first appearance of telescopic forks on a Triumph

passage passed between the cylinder bores and took an elongated cross-section to do this. The carburettor was an Amal. The block was surmounted by a one-piece iron head that held the combustion space above the valve pockets and gave a 5 : 1 compression ratio.

The rest of the machine was stock Triumph except for the front forks, which were telescopics for the first time for the marque. Those aside, it was a case of standard four-speed gearbox, rigid frame and all the usual items, such as tank, seat, wheels and mudguards.

Only one machine was built and according to its designer it was in fact a political exercise carried out to put one over on BSA. For all that it did give a direction and in the fullness of time did become a production military machine, but not until postwar days.

The elements of the design next appeared in 1946 in response to the later Ministry specification and at first looked to be the same in detail.

However, while the engine was still of 500 cc with side valves, the crankshaft used the 3TW design of overhung crankpins clamped into a centre flywheel. The camshaft still ran across the front of the crankcase but was now gear driven with a massive idler connecting the gears on crankshaft, camshaft and magneto. Ignition was thus by the more traditional method and, as always, the oil pump was driven from the end of the camshaft.

Valve lifters were provided and the exhaust ports splayed out and down much more than before. The two pipes just pushed into the ports and fed into a box carried like a conductor's money bag ahead of the crankcase. From this a single pipe ran low down on the right to the silencer. The inlet side remained the same with a tunnel passing through the block and an Amal providing the mixture.

To keep the weight down both head and barrel were in light alloy. No dynamo was fitted, but an alternator went on the left crankshaft end within a dome on the cast alloy chaincase. Inside this a duplex chain drove the clutch and a three-

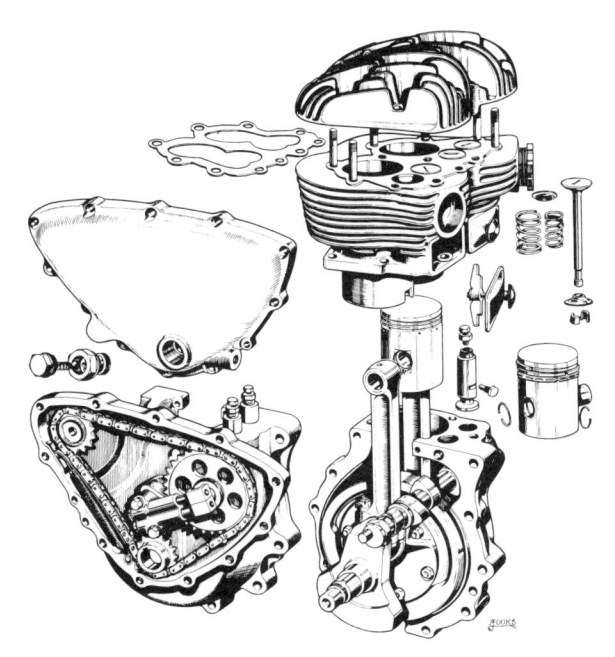

Engine unit of the 5TW showing chain camshaft drive and other details

Below right **TRW engine and curious front silencer box unlikely to survive much off-road use**

Below **Transmission side of the prototype TRW showing the fully enclosed rear chain**

speed gearbox, which was a separate unit, bolted to the rear of the engine. A slipper tensioner kept the primary chain in adjustment and in 1948 the first prototype was fitted with a four-speed gear cluster, while the second kept to three.

The rear chain was fully enclosed by a Rubberoid tube for each run, which joined the gearbox and primary chaincase to a split housing that enclosed the rear wheel sprocket.

The engine unit went into a rigid frame with telescopic front forks. The fuel tank was as on the 350 cc twin, acting as a frame brace; an air cleaner went opposite the oil tank. Thanks to the fairly extensive use of light alloy the weight was a very respectable 280 lb, thus well within the Ministry requirement.

Over the next year or so the Triumph underwent a whole series of tests and was tried with several variations in specification. Thus the tyre section varied from a normal 3·25 in. to a fat 5·0 in. while other carburettors were evaluated.

In all the machine was just what the services needed, but by then the war was over and the military were knee deep in machines they wanted to get rid of. No way was anyone going to sanction the purchase of a new and rather expensive model when thousands of machines lay in dumps awaiting buyers. So the tests continued to keep the project alive and gradually the model became swathed in peace-time Ministry procrastination.

England – more makes than most

83

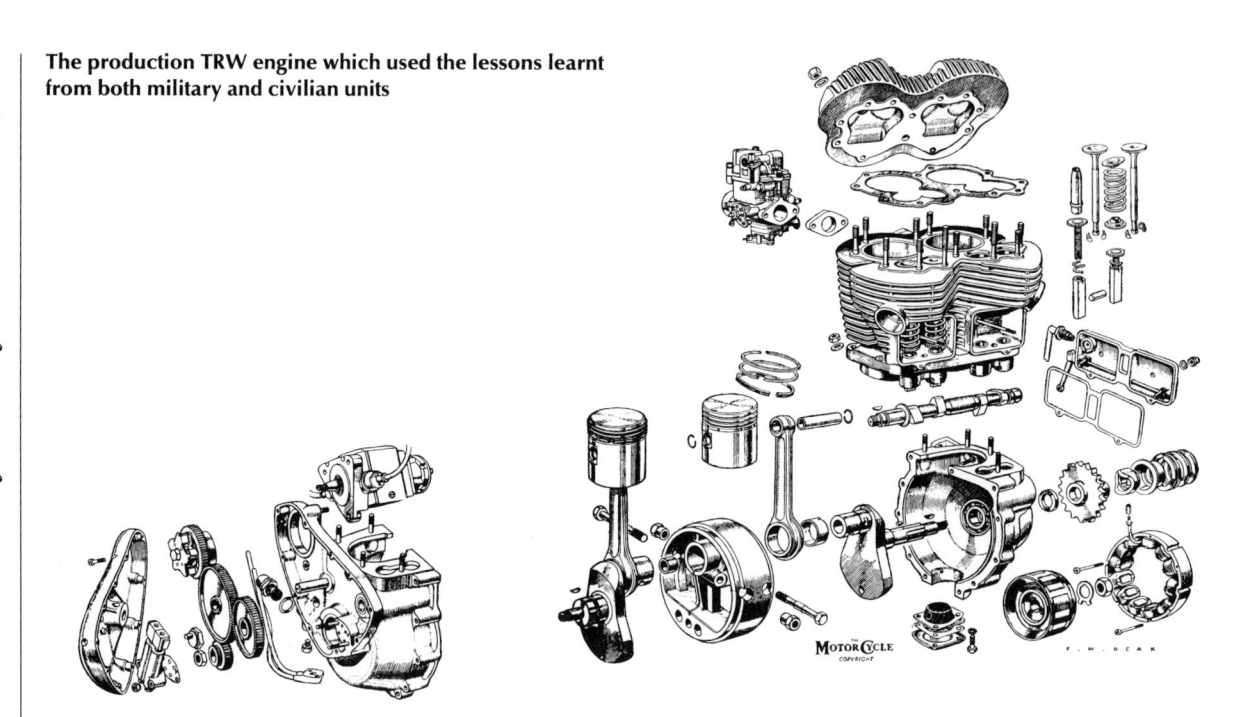

The production TRW engine which used the lessons learnt from both military and civilian units

To cut costs the design was modified to use as many parts from the production line as possible, and from the interminable meetings came the final specification of the postwar military machine, the TRW Triumph. Even then orders were sparse, but they did come for both British and overseas forces and the machine continued to be built up to 1964, by which time some 5700 had been turned out.

The TRW used the engine from the 1946 design with only detail changes to suit its production. It remained an all-alloy unit but with separate standard Triumph four-speed gearbox, and was fitted with a Solex carburettor. The exhausts were still siamesed into one silencer on the right, but without the odd primary chamber in front of the crankcase.

The electrics were altered to alternator, distributor mounted in the old magneto position and coil ignition. This was simple and gave an emergency start, for the machine could be run without a battery and with direct lighting. The magneto was by then obsolete as far as the services were concerned and thus a potential repair problem.

The cycle parts picked out for the TRW came from the firm's TR5 Trophy model. This competition-orientated machine had the frame, forks and wheels best suited to a model destined for at least some off-road use and so provided a good base. With these parts came the Triumph nacelle and tank top grid and to the resulting machine were added panniers and other army items. All told, it was a successful machine until the 1960s, when it was replaced by an overhead-valve machine from Triumph based on the unit construction model.

During the war the Triumph twin engine did other jobs. The most famous was that of driving a portable generator for the RAF. The complete unit had to be light enough to be carried by two men; they would hump it out from hangar to aircraft, where it was fired up and provided the necessary current to start the flying engines.

At first sight the engine chosen for the job seemed to be a standard Speed Twin, but in fact few of the motorcycle parts would fit the generator engine. The first change was to reverse the cylinder head so that the camshafts opened the opposite valves to usual and the magneto was driven from the exhaust one.

The most important feature for postwar riders was the fitting of head and barrel cast in a silicon aluminium alloy with inserts. In the head these were of a high-expansion iron to form the valve seats and plug boss. The cylinder block contained liners with integral lugs at the top to take the head bolts.

To suit the installation the ports, both inlet and exhaust, pointed straight out from the head, and both head and block were cast in a rectangular form with regular finning. This was to suit a cowl attached to the cylinder block by two screws on each side that threaded into small cast bosses, which characterized the postwar engine. The head cowl was attached to the rocker box fixings by nuts.

The cowl was extended round a large magnesium alloy fan fitted to the crankshaft outboard of the timing chest. Its centre incorporated a driving dog for the cranking handle normally used for starting. The fan moved around 400 cu. ft of air per minute at the normal 4000 rpm running speed and more than half of this was ducted over the engine. The rest went to the dynamo, where it passed through vents between the body of the armature and its windings.

The cooling was augmented by using an oil pump of nearly twice the capacity of the motorcycle one and by passing the oil through a Vokes filter on its way back to its tank; a feature to appear after the war on the Grand Prix model. In its turn the oil was cooled by the oil tank being built as the base of the fuel tank with respective capacities of five pints and three gallons.

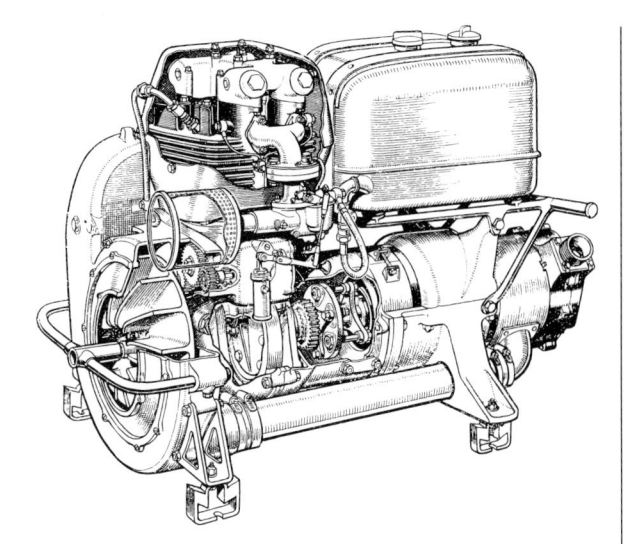

The Triumph generator unit whose head and barrel led to postwar GP and TR5 models

On the exhaust side the two pipes joined into one and connected to a single tubular silencer that ran along the unit. The inlet was a little more complicated as it included a governor driven by the inlet camshaft in the manner of the motorcycle dynamo. The governor used outflung ball bearings working against a regulating spring to hold the set engine speed to a close tolerance. In the linkage was a dashpot connected to the throttle of the updraught Zenith carburettor, which supplied the mixture to both barrels. A Vokes air filter kept it clean.

Between the engine and the dynamo went a flexible coupling and built into this was a ratchet mechanism and a gear. This was used with a kickstart and quadrant that could be bolted in place if needed.

The complete assembly measured $30\frac{1}{2}$ in. long, $23\frac{3}{4}$ in. high and $17\frac{1}{2}$ in. wide. It weighed 175 lb dry, so with petrol and oil really was quite a load for two men to carry any distance, even when propelled by the workshop sergeant. Thus most were mounted in a light two-wheeled trailer along with switchgear and leads for connecting to the aircraft.

Examples were also built in a fully enclosed form for fitting inside aircraft to supply all ancillary current. The low weight was again a useful feature and postwar the top half alloy castings were used for both the Trophy and Grand Prix models. The latter was made in no other form than the first prototype, which won the Manx GP, but the TR5 was later fitted with the die-cast head and barrel also used for the Tiger 100.

The generator units were still to be seen in the RAF into the mid-1950s, but by then workshop personnel had become suspicious of them. Unlike the normal low-speed stationary engines they used, the generator had zip. It fired up as if it meant action and a blip on the throttle sent it up the scale and brought the NCO running to close it down.

Postwar, the military Triumph 3HW was very popular for spares were plentiful, the machine strongly made and the engine receptive to tuning. Many were quickly modified for competition and proved successful for a good few years until something more purpose-built came along.

Velocette

The idea of entrusting the Velocette clutch with its strange design and adjustment myth and lore to service personnel is enough to make any enthusiast for the marque cringe. If that was not enough, the first order came from the French, so the entire ritual had to be translated for the handbook.

One might be forgiven for thinking that it was provident that the first batch were lost *en route* to France and that before any more were ready that country had fallen and machine production halted at Hall Green for a while. Aside from the clutch, the Velocette single had other idiosyncrasies beloved by owner but treated with suspicion by all other riders.

At the start of the war Velocette had just begun production of their 1940 range, but were soon switched to service contracts, mainly for high-precision parts. One that was a little less

The Velocette MDD model as built in the early years of the war and based on the MAC

Drive side of the later Velocette MAF with revised frame, brake pedal and footrest

MAF timing side showing direct gear pedal linkage and folding kickstart lever

demanding was to paint steel helmets. No War Office order for motorcycles appeared, but the French one did – for 1200 machines.

With the first batch lost and the French out of the picture the firm looked to the English authorities to take the bulk of the machines, but it was some time before this happened and it was on the understanding that no more would be required. Later the situation changed and, although the firm was by then very busy with war material production, it was called on to produce more machines.

These were based on the same model, but before going into production with it the opportunity was taken to incorporate some changes to make it more suited to service use. In comparison with some of the other motorcycle firms, production was small, amounting to some 20 machines a week, and in all the firm produced about 5000 motorcycles during the war years. Near the end of the war production was halted, although spares were still required for a time, and then the company became involved in rebuilds of War Department machines.

The wartime machines were all based on the prewar MAC model with a single cylinder high camshaft engine of 68 × 96 mm dimensions and 349 cc capacity. Construction was unique to Velocette, with a very narrow crankcase that extended well up the cylinder with the timing chest on the right. The camshaft was gear driven from an idler meshed with the crankshaft and itself drove the magneto gear. Above the cams went a pair of trailing bell-cranks and these moved the pushrods, which were both enclosed within a single tube that reached up to the light alloy rocker box, which fully enclosed the valve gear. The valves were restrained by coil springs.

Both head and barrel were in iron and were held on with studs, while in the lower half the crankshaft was built up with a caged roller big end. The oil pump was gear driven from the right crankend and fitted in below the timing chest. This was enclosed by a single cover, normally cast in light alloy, but later in the war when this was in short supply cast iron was used.

The magneto was tucked in behind the cylinder, but the dynamo was clamped to the front of the crankcase and driven by belt from the left end of the crankshaft. Inboard of the pulley went the engine sprocket, close up to the crankcase wall, and it drove the clutch via a chain within a pressed steel case. The narrow crankcase went with the clutch position inboard

England – more makes than most

87

of the final drive sprocket and from that position the design and layout of the lift mechanism came that made it so special. The gearbox was otherwise a straightforward, four-speed foot-change unit that was special only in the direction of its pedal movement, which was up for up, and that the power went in on the sleeve gear and out on the mainshaft – in reverse to the normal English arrangement.

The first wartime batch, originally for the French, was typed MDD and used the standard frame and forks with just the addition of a crankcase shield bolted to the underside of the frame. Other modifications included lower overall gearing with a lower first gear ratio as well, a sturdier clutch and a lower compression ratio to suit the poor fuel available.

A standard Velocette in use in Australia ridden by messengers of the National Emergency Services

The later models were the MAF, and this nomenclature was to be appropriate as some of the machines went to the RAF. The machines received further changes, one of which was a much neater connection between gear lever and box to reverse the change sequence to up for down. This brought the machine into line with the rest of the makes used by the services and saved numerous layshafts from untimely breakage caused by riders forgetting and changing the wrong way.

To save light alloy the gearbox end cover was cast in iron along with some other details. The kickstart lever was modified from a folding pedal to a folding one-piece pedal and crank. This turned in a hefty boss on the spindle and was less prone to rattle.

The frame was altered to incorporate a substantial member beneath the crankcase and this ran well back and presented a smooth surface to the ground. The forks had rubber bump stops added to the rear tubes positioned to hit the lower crown on full deflection. While amending the frame the chance was taken to give the rear brake pedal its own mounting lug and to tuck it inside the footrest to be more out of harm's way.

On the standard models the rear brake torque bolt was a heavily stressed item that just had to be kept tight, so this was changed for a torque stay, which ran from the lower edge of the backplate to the prop stand lug and reduced rear frame loads. The prop stand itself was short but efficient and backed up front and rear stands, the rear held by a clip.

The rear chain was very well shrouded on both top and bottom runs, and the model was fitted out in the usual service style with panniers, rear carrier, sometimes a pillion seat and headlamp mask. The silencer was a poor thing by Velocette standards being tubular, but it did retain the traditional fishtail.

In all a model that was highly regarded by those lucky enough to ride one – but they were few in number compared with BSA or Norton. Very few survived and some were among the machines returned to the works for rebuilding. During this process they lost their MAF identity and emerged in MAC style in the normal Velocette black and gold. Thus the ranks of MAF models were further decimated to make them a rare model.

Welbike

The Welbike was the most special of the machines used by paratroops, as one prime requirement was that it had to fit into a cylindrical container no more than 15 in. in diameter. This would then be dropped by parachute and the bike had to be ready for immediate action straight from its crate.

The problem was solved by Lieutenant-Colonel J. R. V. Dolphin, who designed a suitable model with small wheels and fold-down parts to enable it to fit its container. Really small wheels would not have been too good an idea for use on the tracks and paths near the front, so the largest practical tyre that would fit in the space was chosen and these gave an acceptable rolling diameter.

A Welbike in use on an airfield in Bengal in 1944. They proved ideal for such work

The model name came from the designer's home town, Welwyn, and the machine was really reduced to the bare necessities. It was strictly intended for brief use, after which it became expendable, so comfort was of no importance especially as it was only to be used by fit, trained young men from parachute or front-line regiments. It was taken as read that they were tough and would accept the basic nature of the bike.

To suit the small build a laid-down engine was needed, and the Villiers Junior De Luxe unit was chosen as being both available and suitable. This was a simple two-stroke of 98 cc with 50 mm bore and stroke and was made in one with a clutch and reduction ratio.

Engine construction was very simple and based on an overhung crankshaft running in a main crankcase that extended back to form the clutch chamber. It supported one main bearing and its cover held the second, while between them was keyed the drive sprocket. Outside the cover went a flywheel magneto.

The crankshaft had a roller big end and the connecting rod supported a flat top piston that ran in an iron barrel. This had twin exhausts on its sides and to these were fitted cast light alloy manifolds, which carried the gases down to an alloy silencer mounted below the engine unit. The carburettor went on the left on an inlet stub.

The cylinder head was in light alloy and positioned to the barrel with the plug laying out to the right and the matching compression release to the left. Bolts secured the head and nuts the barrel, which went on to the main crankcase; a cover bolted to its right side to seal the case chamber.

A shaft ran across the unit behind the crankcase proper and carried the clutch. This was chain driven, lifted by a lever on the left, and drove the output sprocket keyed on to the shaft on the left side.

The frame comprised four tubes arranged to run past the engine unit as two pairs. They came

Military Motorcycles of World War 2

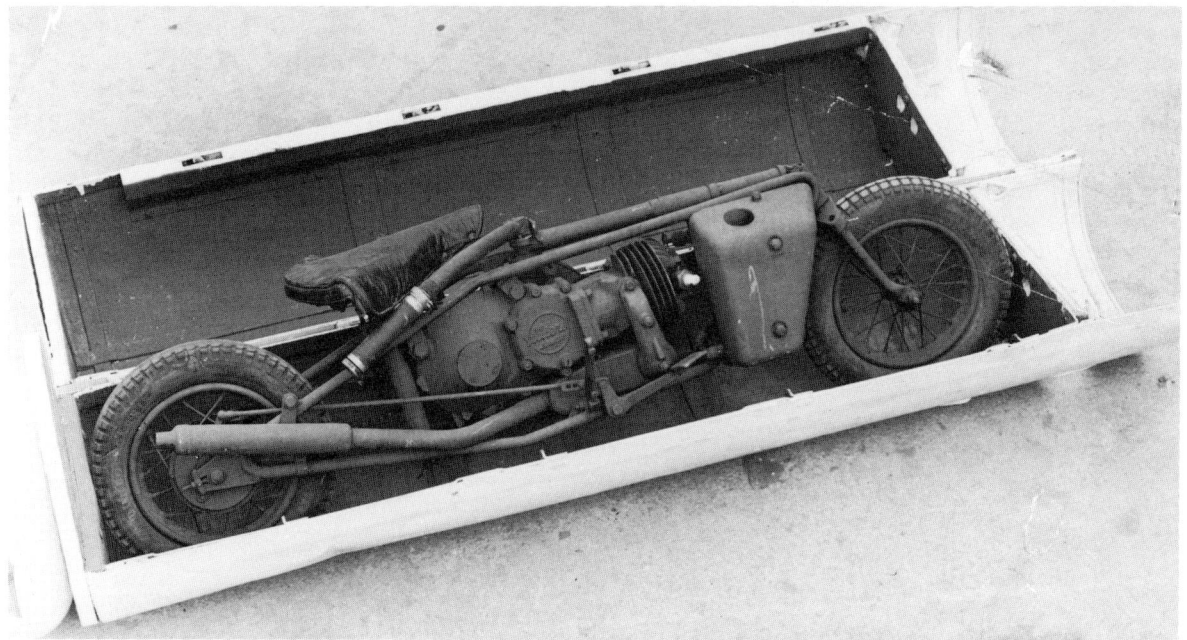

90

Left **Welbike in its drop canister folded down to fit**

Below left **Right side of machine showing the engine, silencer and single brake**

together at headstock and rear wheel spindle to support these items. A bicycle front fork was deemed adequate and carried the simple front wheel. The rear one had a drum brake, which was operated by a foot pedal on the right. This was the rider's sole means of stopping other than baling out. Tyre size was $12\frac{1}{2} \times 2\frac{1}{4}$ in.

The handlebars folded down and the footrests up, while the seat pillar slid into a tube welded into the frame. Twin pannier fuel tanks were bolted one each side of the frame ahead of the engine and because their feed was below the level of the float chamber they had to be pressurized to ensure the petrol reached the engine. This was done with a handpump mounted between the left tank and the exposed flywheel magneto.

Thus, on landing, the case clips were knocked back and the machine lifted out. The footrests fell down and the seat was pulled up and locked with a catch. The handlebars were raised and held firm by knurled nuts and the tank pumped up. Flood the carb, paddle off with decompressor raised and then away the machine went to carry man and gun.

The Welbike was made by the motorcycle firm Excelsior and this caused some confusion after the war when the Corgi model appeared. This was a civilian version of the Welbike and used an Excelsior Spryt engine in place of the wartime Villiers unit, but was not built by the Tyseley firm. Instead, the Corgi was made by Brockhouse of Southport, who built the engine under licence.

During the war the Welbike was built in two forms, Series 1 and 2, but the differences were in details only. The first Series numbered nearly 1200, but the other was reputed to total over 10,000, of which 8000 were sold off after the war. Rumour has it that they went to Macy's in New York, maybe the smallest machine for the biggest store, but as the Corgi it stayed in production until 1954.

6 France – six makes or more

Britain and France stood together to present the ultimatum to Germany to withdraw from Poland. So together they went to war and in the early weeks French troops advanced into Germany and British servicemen were moved to France.

During the closing weeks of 1939 and the early months of 1940 the status quo remained. Then in April Norway and Denmark were invaded by Germany, followed in May by the lightning advance through the Low Countries and into France. June brought the Dunkirk evacuation, the appearance of Italy at Germany's side and an armistice in France.

The terms split France in two, leaving the unoccupied territory under the Vichy government, to the distress of the Free French forces and patriotic Frenchmen everywhere. The occupied area was set to work on behalf of the German war machine and over the next two years skilled French workers were recruited to go to German factories. The response was not encouraging. Late in 1942 the rest of the country was taken over, although this made little real difference to events.

And so it was with motorcycles, with the machines of the French army being taken over and used by the Wehrmacht.

In the late 1930s the French motorcycle industry was producing an extensive range of ma-

A line of French Terrot machines which were with a Polish brigade which moved from Syria to Palestine to join up with British troops

chines for its home market, but few went to other countries. The models included two-strokes from 100 to 250 cc and four-strokes up to one litre, with the larger models vee or flat twins. Valves were at the side or overhead and, while many machines were constructed on English lines, most had Gallic style.

A number of the more prosaic were used by the French army for general duties and makes seen included Terrot, Motobecane, Peugeot and

Monet et Goyon. Better known were sidecar outfits from Gnome et Rhone and Rene Gillet.

The Gnome et Rhone model was based on a pair of flat twins in the 1938 range which were of 500 and 750 cc capacity with overhead valves.

Gnome et Rhone flat twin machines used solo and with sidecar in May 1940

For the service the firm produced the 750 Armée, which was more heavily constructed and propelled by an 804 cc flat twin, side-valve engine coupled to a four-speed gearbox, which drove both rear and sidecar wheels by shaft.

Engine construction followed normal lines for the type with the camshaft above the crankshaft and the electrics above that. Wet sump lubrication was used and both induction and exhaust followed convention. The gearbox was controlled by a rocking pedal on the right which was linked to a positive stop mechanism mounted on top of the box. The shaft to the rear wheel was exposed and on the right, while the transverse kickstart pedal went on the left.

The frame was built up from steel pressings, as was normal to Gnome et Rhone, with the fuel tank set between the upper members. At the rear the two sides terminated in round areas and the bevel box bolted to that on the right. The front forks were pressed steel blade girders controlled by rubber links, and both wheels had good-sized drum brakes.

A saddle was provided for the driver and behind this went a rear carrier on the mudguard. A pannier bag was fitted either side of this and each was shaped to the mudguard line and its stays. A headlight hung well out in front of the forks so was little protected from damage. The speedometer was set in the front of the tank with the filler cap behind it. Long, swept-back handlebars were fitted and there were footboards and footrests, which gave the driver a choice of positions to rest his feet.

The sidecar fitted to the AX2, as the flat twin was typed, was a single seater carrying a spare wheel on its tail. There was no screen, but a *tonneau* and door cover were supplied to give the passenger some protection from the weather. The sidecar chassis used varied, with some built more heavily than others for towing purposes.

Outfits made at Gnome et Rhone, used by the German army and liberated in 1944. The censor has painted out all visible unit markings

The bodies also varied in detail fittings, with some carrying machine guns plus ammunition cases, others hand grenades or extra fuel or supplies.

The French army also used Rene Gillet V-twins of 750 and 1000 cc to haul sidecars and men along. These were of conventional form with side-valve engines and all-chain drive via a crossover gearbox. The frame was tubular and rigid, while the front forks were of a short leading link design favoured by the marque. They comprised a fixed girder fork with the links pivoted at the bottom to carry the wheel. From the front of the links a member shaped like a bicycle fork took the wheel movement to springs anchored to the top crown.

Many sidecar outfits of both Gnome et Rhone and Rene Gillet manufacture were captured by the Germans, often repainted, given new unit markings and then used fairly extensively by the Wehrmacht. It was experience with them together with the Belgian outfits that led to the specialized German models.

7 | Germany – not just flat twins

The German motorcycle industry was prepared with Teutonic thoroughness as part of an overall plan that was aimed to use everyone and everything available to promote party aims. As the aims included using force when and where heavy persuasion failed, the military had first choice of equipment and this included two wheelers.

Long before war came the Nazi party was working hard to promote Germany and to increase her share of the world's markets. To this end they exported below cost and paid for this with a levy on all home business down to the smallest trader. This tax helped to fund the very large sums spent on propaganda of all kinds, which included car and motorcycle sport.

So the world saw and was very impressed by the Mercedes-Benz and Auto Union cars, which swept all before them. On two wheels matters did not turn out quite so well, despite the sophisticated designs and teams of mechanics. Three makes were involved, these being BMW, NSU and DKW. The first raced in the 500 cc class and had a very successful 1938 season, but was less fortunate the following year, when they won the TT but found that the Gilera four had the legs of them in many events.

The 250 cc class was the province of DKW and the blown two-strokes dominated their class in the late 1930s, with the Italian Guzzi and Benelli machines seldom getting ahead except at the TT. The 350 cc class was down to NSU and in this area things went awry. The complex blown twins were neither reliable nor fast enough so DKW were called upon to take over. They could not hold Velocette in 1938 but in 1939 tied with the English machine over the shortened season, so had done a fair job.

While this promotion was going on on a grand scale the German industry was being organized and streamlined for economical production. The motorcycle was considered important to Germany as it made a most effective use of materials in its construction and fuel in its operation, so large numbers of lightweights were built and their use was encouraged. This gave the population mobility at low cost, but more important to the State was the large number of people who thereby became experienced both in the riding and the repair of motorcycles.

The German army was turning to the motor vehicle for rapid transport of men and arms to the front and could thus draw on this experience when mobilization called the men to arms. Many of the motorsport organizations for civilians required their members to train on military equipment, so a ready source of personnel was to hand.

The industry was rationalized late in 1938 by Colonel Oberst von Schell, later General, who was given complete power of the type only available in a totalitarian State. His orders were to change the industry to the greatest practical extent in order that it would be of the fullest use

A rider from a German medical unit riding back through British lines after surrendering in a key Dutch town. His machine is believed to be an early thirties Rudge

to the country in the event of war. He therefore carefully cut back on types of vehicles, motorcycles and component parts.

150 motorcycle types became 30 and were built by nine companies. In addition there would be 41 small firms making autocycles most of whom used an engine from one of two companies. Firms were not given a choice but were told the type of machine they would be allowed to build and how many had to be produced.

It was in the parts that the greatest reduction in numbers of types were made and 25 electric horns, ten number plates, 20 autocycle pedalling gears and some 60 pillion seats were all reduced to just one of each. There were two types of clutch lining and tyre pump and three saddles

When heiling was good for your health. Plenty of flags out also

1942 and reality in Russian mud during the push towards Stalingrad. Machine is a BMW

in place of 22. Inside the engine 57 piston assemblies came down to eight.

Hubs went from 25 to nine, wheels from 200 to nine, spokes from 40 to 13 and footrests from 150 to nine, presumably on the basis that 'you riders vill put your feet where ve tell you'.

All told it was a remarkable reduction with very considerable cost benefits and of great help to military stores holdings. In addition to this and the gradual elimination of the smaller firms, the dealers were also taken down in numbers. Those left were allocated particular machines to service and hold spares for while the rest could always find a job in uniform servicing Wehrmacht machines.

During the war the German machines followed more than one trend. They began with solos that ranged from tiny two-strokes to big flat twins, which also were coupled to a sidecar. These lacked sidecar wheel drive, and observation of the Belgian FN and its abilities under arduous conditions led to the complex BMW and Zundapp combinations. These were, however, expensive to build. Then just after the middle of 1944 their production was stopped, for the Germans found that their military Volkswagen was better, cheaper and much easier to build. Just as the Allies found with the Jeep. Thus for the last few months of the war German production was of 125 and 350 cc DKW models.

At the end of the war some of the industry lay in ruins but other areas were able to get going again. Times were very difficult, for the country was split into zones, everything was in short supply and the motorcycle industry was restricted, at first to not making powered two wheelers and then by capacity.

Then came Marshall Aid, the Berlin airlift and the division of the country into East and West. East of the line were the old DKW works, which became MZ and part of BMW. In the West the Germans created their Economic Miracle.

Ardie

This firm was founded just after World War I and built its own two-strokes and later models using JAP engines. In the 1930s it turned to German engines and just before World War 2 produced a line of two-strokes using its own and Bark or Fichtel & Sachs engines.

For the Wehrmacht they built two machines, both straightforward two-strokes and both based on their civilian range. The machines were of 125 and 200 cc capacity with an inclined single-cylinder engine with twin exhausts. The design was advanced and the engines included a squish band feature, alloy head, alloy barrel with iron liner and through-bolt retention of head and barrel. The cylinder finned length was short, for the spigot extended well into the crankcase, and the ports were arranged with the exhausts to each side and a transfer front and rear.

The exhausts fed into rear-facing pipes with high-rise silencers on the civilian 125 and low on the 200. The inlet fed into the side of the cylinder on the 200 and the rear on the 125 under piston control.

The three-speed gearbox was built in unit with the engine and on the 125 was driven by a clutch on the end of the crankshaft. That model had its final drive chain on the right but on the 200 it was on the left.

Both models had rigid tubular frames with pressed steel blade girder front forks. Drum brakes were fitted and the remainder of the machines was conventional. The battery went aft of the cylinder and the usual road equipment was fitted plus Wehrmacht additions.

Over 9000 of the 125 were built from 1939 to 1943 and most of these went to the army. Towards the end of the war much of their machining plant was moved into cellars in and around Nuremberg and there put to work to produce aircraft parts, so motorcycle production lapsed.

After the war it was recovered and for a short while the 125 was built for the Ordnance Department of the US army, but in time the firm went back to its two-stroke production for civilians.

BMW

BMW are known first and foremost as makers of motorcycles with flat twin engines and shaft drive so it is not surprising that their best-known wartime model would have these two features. This was the R75, also well known for its dual range and reverse gearbox, locking differential and sidecar wheel drive.

The R75 was preceded by the R12 and these two flat twins were accompanied by a pair of single-cylinder solos also used extensively by the Wehrmacht and the Luftwaffe. In addition to the four main models the services also used other versions of the flat twin and some of these may well have been impressed from civilian sources.

The oldest model used was the single-cylinder R4, which dated back to 1932. As with all BMWs it was of unit construction with the crankshaft axis laid along the machine driving the clutch. Behind that went the gearbox and from that came the drive shaft on the right to the rear bevel box and wheel.

The 398 cc engine had overhead valves with the pushrods working in separate tunnels on the left. The electrics went to the front of the unit and the carburettor to the rear. The exhaust ran down to a silencer on the left.

With the gearbox built-in unit it made for a neat assembly, the gearchange being by a hand lever, which sprouted from its top. It was a car-type change and the lever ran up to pass through the right kneegrip in which was the gate for the four speeds. It was thus possible to go directly into neutral from any gear.

The drive shaft had a universal joint at its front end and ran fully exposed. The bevel box was attached to the frame by a ring of bolts and also carried the rear brake shoes with the cam lever on the right and convenient for connecting to the brake pedal on the same side.

The frame was old fashioned and built up from channel-section pressings welded together. It was rigid and was a full duplex cradle comprising two side assemblies held in place by cross members and the steering head. They thus spanned the engine unit with the lower run and the fuel tank with the upper.

The old fashioned R4 BMW with pressed steel frame, trailing link forks and car type gear lever

The front forks were equally old and used the short trailing link principle from the original BMW twin of 1923. Curved pressed steel blades carried the short links and these carried the wheel. The suspension medium was a short quarter-elliptic spring bolted to the underside of the steering head so that it pointed forward. From its front end a loop ran down to the wheel spindle and thus transferred wheel movement to the spring. A friction damper was fitted on the right side.

For the rest the tank was set in the frame and the saddle, a rather small and thin item, was suspended by coil springs working in tension in vintage fashion. A centre stand pivoted under the frame and a crankcase shield was added at the front. A rear carrier was normally fitted and panniers hung on each side. A pillion seat and rests could be added if need be.

The second single was the R35, which was introduced in 1937 and could be considered as a replacement for the R4. It was very similar but with a reduced bore, which gave a capacity of 342 cc. There were detail changes to the electrics, but in most other respects the engine and transmission followed the earlier lines.

The cycle parts also stayed as they were but with one notable exception – the front forks. These became telescopics and the front wheel, mudguard and headlight were changed to suit. The forks were not the impressive ones fitted to the twins but a lighter version, with gaiters at their lower ends, and no hydraulics.

The service edition was given a drab finish in place of the normal black with white lining and its equipment included a headlamp mask and the inevitable panniers. The hefty sump guard was continued.

Latter R35 which replaced the R4 and was fitted with lightweight telescopic forks

Military Motorcycles of World War 2

The first of the flat twins – used in very large numbers – was the R12. This model was introduced in 1935 and its front suspension represented a great step forward for it was by telescopic forks with hydraulic damping. This was a world first for such a system, although the Danish Nimbus must have run it close.

For the rest the frame continued as built-up steel pressings with a rigid rear end and with the fuel tank set between the upper members. The army retained the civilian footboards at first and had a rather extensive front mudguard later changed for a simpler one. Panniers were fitted and a pillion seat with springing was bolted on top of the rear carrier. A passenger handle was incorporated in the front of the assembly, which sat the user some way above the driver, from which perch he could act as lookout.

The engine unit was of 745 cc with side valves and square engine dimensions of 78 × 78 mm. A single carburettor supplied both barrels via inlet tracts and the exhausts ran back low down on each side. Construction of the engine and gearbox followed BMW tradition with the magneto and dynamo mounted on top of the crankcase, wet sump lubrication and engine speed clutch. The gearbox contained four speeds

Left **The first BMW with telescopic forks, the R12 flat twin in army guise. Note footboards for both rider and passenger**

Below left **A captured BMW R75 undergoing investigation in England during 1945**

Rear view of R75 which shows the drive to the sidecar wheel and the large transmission housing by the rear wheel

Military Motorcycles of World War 2

104

and used the car gate-type handchange, while the final drive shaft went on the right. The saddle continued with its vintage-style springs.

Most military R12 models were used with a sidecar fitted and the gearing lowered to suit. The sidecar was a stark single-seater designed for the emergencies of wartime rather than the comforts of peace. The body was thus functional and without screen or door to impede entry or egress. It had a grab handle in front of the passenger and a spare wheel could be mounted on top of the deck behind the seat. This area also provided some stowage space for rations, schnapps or ammunition depending on the driver's preferences.

The R12 had a limited power output of 18 bhp in single carburettor form and in the mud of Flanders the Germans found that this was either not enough to drag the weight of machine and many passengers along or it gave them wheelspin. During this campaign they came across examples of the FN with sidecar wheel drive and decided to exploit this idea themselves.

BMW and Zundapp were the two firms chosen to do this and worked together on development and production so that some items were interchangeable. The BMW was the R75 and the engine was on the lines of the SV R71 but with several changes and ohv heads. The compression ratio was 5·8:1 and on this modest figure the ohv engine produced 26 bhp at 4000 rpm. Twin 24 mm Graetzin carburettors supplied the mixture and were connected to a single air cleaner. In the first year of production this was mounted on top of the gearbox, but problems with Russian mud covering it totally meant that a larger filter went on top of the petrol tank. The

Schnapps holder in the Steib sidecar fitted to the R75 BMW and Zundapp KS750, here with the first of these machines

domed cover held a removable element and had a choke built into it and worked by a lever protruding to one side.

The exhaust was also a little special with the two cylinders connecting to a cylindrical silencer box mounted in front of the crankcase sump. From this a pipe ran back low down on the right to the rear bevel box, where it turned up to enter the centre of a high-mounted silencer. This was a rear outlet and was fitted with a perforated heat shield to protect the rider.

For the Russian front in 1943 the exhaust was altered to pass through a heat exchanger; the warm air from this ducted over the rider's feet, his hands and into the sidecar. It went some way to combating the bitter cold.

Ignition was by magneto and both it and the camshaft were driven by gears at the front of the engine. A pancake dynamo went on the crankshaft nose with its cut-out mounted on top of its cover. The lubrication system was wet sump with a gear pump as normal on a BMW.

The clutch had the usual single plate, but from then on the transmission was special. The gearbox contained four ratios plus a two-speed set to give high or low gearing and a reverse gear. Control of all these was by a foot pedal on the

Above left **R75 in factory smart condition; they soon wore a mud coat in action**

Left **Right side of R75 with sidecar removed to show machine details**

Two civilian BMW flat twins being used by the British army. Nearest machine is an R51 and the other an R66

left and two hand levers working in and beside a gate bolted to the right of the tank. The inner lever was protected by a button set in its top and selected the direction of travel while the outer one looked after the high and low choice.

From the gearbox an exposed shaft on the right took the drive to the rear bevel box, which was a far more complex assembly than usual. In addition to the normal bevel pair there were ten more spur gears with eight built into a differential unit that split the drive power between rear and sidecar wheels in a ratio to suit their loads and the outfit's centre of gravity. Thanks to this it drove straight ahead under normal circumstances.

For abnormal times the differential could be locked using a lever under the saddle. This slid a dog clutch on the sidecar drive shaft into engagement with the diff cage attached to the back of the crown wheel.

The final pair of gears in the bevel box were from the crown wheel axis back to the rear wheel to help give sidecar wheel offset. The drive across the chassis went to a further pair carried in the sidecar wheel housing, and in this case the drive went forward to further increase the offset.

The wheel housing was able to pivot about the drive shaft and the shaft housing acted as a torsion spring to give the wheel suspension movement. A rubber-covered lug on the frame controlled the extent of this between two ears formed in the back of the housing. A coupling at the bevel box allowed the drive to be parted to allow the sidecar to be removed when needed. The final special transmission detail was that the kickstarter swung in an arc along the machine and used bevel gears to connect to the engine. It thus differed from the standard machines with their transverse levers.

The frame was substantial and built up from tubing and pressings bolted together. It assembled into a full cradle with duplex rails beneath the engine and in front of it. There was no rear suspension as this would have complicated the drive even further, but heavy telescopics went at the front. These had normal fork shrouds up to 1943, after which gaiters were fitted.

All three wheels had very heavy-gauge straight spokes to withstand the load and cornering stresses. They could be interchanged and a spare was commonly carried on the sidecar tail panel. Tyre size was 4·50 × 16 in. with block pattern treads and all three wheels were braked. The rear and sidecar brakes were coupled and operated hydraulically by a single pedal on the left. This moved the piston of a master cylinder, which was bolted to the underside of an extension of the gearbox casting. The front brake was cable operated, with the wire entering the backplate and coupling to a balance linkage between the shoes. Thus there was no external mechanism to catch on bushes and no cam internally.

Both front and rear wheels were shielded by large mudguards with lifting handles and one of the front stays doubled as a stand. At the rear the guard tail would hinge up to let the wheel roll out. The seating was German in style with a large saddle pivoted at its nose and supported by a single vertical coil spring. The pillion seat and its associated grab handle was made as an assembly that could be removed from the rear carrier if so desired.

The fuel tank held 24 litres and before the air filter was moved to this place a toolbox was set in its top, as was common BMW practice for many years. The battery went low down on the left behind the cylinder and the headlight shell carried the lights switch and speedometer.

The sidecar chassis may have been sophisticated but the body was strictly functional. It was suspended on leaf springs and resembled a trials or ISDT type, but in a heavier and sturdier form.

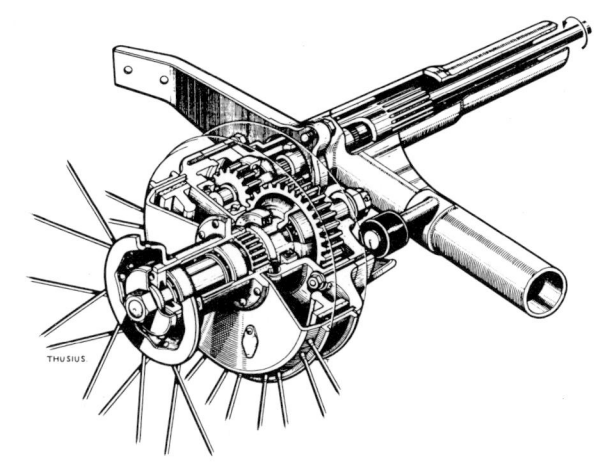

The sidecar wheel drive used by the R75, designed to give the wheel lead and suspension movement

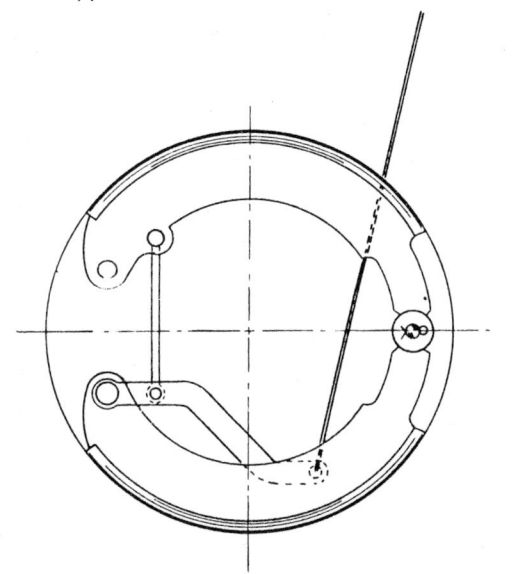

Both BMW and Zundapp used this design of front brake without cam

A crash bar protected the sidecar wheel and matched one fitted to the machine frame to keep the left cylinder from being clouted by any passing Panzers.

The passenger was provided with a seat of a rather basic nature and a grab handle to hold on to. There was no screen of course, but a *tonneau* and a door in the same fabric were available and served to enclose the riding area and any goods the men liked to stow in it. There was also a luggage boot in the tail of the body with access available by hinging up the lid complete with the spare wheel, if this was mounted.

The body nose carried more fittings and it was usual for a pannier to be slung on each side of it. In them would go ammunition, spares, a radio or cold comforts when on the Russian front. On top of the nose was a favourite point to mount a machine gun, but behind the lines a convoy light was more usual. For long-range desert use extra petrol was carried in what became known as 'jerricans', and with a pair of these and a full tank the outfit had a range of around 800 km.

The complete outfit weighed 420 kg unladen and a good deal more when fully fuelled, armed and ready to roll. It thus needed its reverse gear when parking or in tight traffic or other situations.

The R75 served on many fronts and in skilled hands was an excellent means of rapidly crossing

R75 combat ready and demonstrating just how much gear it could carry. A properly restored machine

the countryside. It was also expensive to make and required special training to get the best from it. In the hands of the normal soldier it could became a liability and so in 1944 the Germans turned away from it to light solos and their Kubelwagen, just as the Allies used the Jeep.

In addition to the military BMW models the German services used a number of the more standard twins in various sizes. The oldest and smallest was the R5, which in 1936 had been the first machine in their range to move from the old pressed steel frame to a tubular one. With the telescopic forks introduced the year before the appearance was transformed and stayed much the same for two decades.

The R5 was a typical BMW flat twin with ohv. The engine unit was very smooth, with covers enclosing the electrics and flowed back into the clutch and four-speed gearbox. Twin carburettors helped to produce 24 bhp at 5800 rpm and both foot and hand gear levers were fitted. It was a sales gimmick to offer the so-called 'combined selection of gears by foot or hand controls'.

The R5 cycle parts were mainly new to suit the tubular frame and followed a sober line that was typical of the make and the thinking behind it. In 1938 it became the R51, with a change to plunger rear suspension and a modified drive shaft to accommodate the wheel movement. In this form it was also used by the services, and for them was drab finished and fitted with panniers and headlamp mask.

As well as the 500 the army used a pair of 600s and a 750. The smaller pair were the R61 and R66. The first had a side-valve engine in the tubular plunger frame while the latter had ohv in the same cycle parts. The R66 produced 30 bhp and 5300 rpm so was quite a quick machine, with around 90 mph being claimed.

Finally there was the R71, which took the place of the R12. It had the 745 cc side-valve engine uprated a little to produce 22 bhp at 4600 rpm, and this was installed in the plunger frame as used by the R51 and R61. It was the last side-valve model BMW were to produce and was unusual in that it retained the old-style change with the gate attached to the right side of the tank.

Thus BMW produced one of the most complex and interesting machines of the period, but in the end the simple single proved to be a more useful motorcycle and four wheels more suited to carrying bulk.

DKW

During the 1930s DKW led the world in the exploitation of the supercharged split single and with that layout enjoyed many racing successes. By the end of that period they had also learned to use the Schnurle scavenging system to improve the power output of their road engines without the complication of the racing ones.

Of the models they built for the services the smallest was destined to become the most copied machine of all, for postwar the RT125 became in time the BSA Bantam, Harley-Davidson Hummer, Yamaha YA1 or Red Dragonfly and Moskva 125 (from Russia). This last because the factory found itself in East Germany in 1945, and in time it became Ifa and then Motorradwerke Zschopau or MZ. It continued to lead the world in two-stroke innovative design for many years.

For the German army in 1939 the RT125 was a nice light means of transport for one soldier and ideal for work behind the lines, carrying messages and items from place to place. It was powered by a 123 cc two-stroke engine using a 25 : 1 petroil mixture, with single cylinder, piston-controlled inlet and three-speed gearbox built in unit with it. The cylinder head was in light alloy and the barrel in cast iron. It spigoted deep into the vertically split crankcase and the crankshaft was built up with a roller big end.

The transmission was by primary chain on the left to the cross-over drive gearbox, with the final drive chain on the right. Gearchange and kick-

The RT125 as built by the originators, DKW, and which proved so popular postwar with other names on the tank

start pedals went on concentric spindles on the left.

The engine unit went into a simple tubular cradle frame with blade girder front forks and no rear suspension. The wheels were spoked and had small drum brakes and 2·50 × 19 in. tyres front and rear. The saddle had two springs at the rear and behind it went a small carrier. The battery went under the seat with the horn beside it on the right and full lighting equipment was fitted.

For the Wehrmacht a pair of metal panniers were mounted to either side of the rear wheel. These were smaller than usual so were well clear of the rear wheel spindle and the exhaust system, which ran low down on the right. A tyre pump was clipped to the frame front downtube.

Two further two-stroke singles were used by the services, these being the NZ250 and NZ350. The latter was the more common and from mid-1944 on was, with the RT125, the only military machine kept in production. The two NZ machines were very similar but based on different bores and crankshafts. The smaller used square 68 × 68 mm dimensions but the larger was a long stroke at 72 × 85 mm. Both ran at a peak of 4000 rpm and their construction was very much as the RT125. From 1941 only the 350 was continued, in a modified form with cast iron crankcase and covers, the same modifications were also carried out on the 125.

Differences were in detail, with the rear sparking plug of the 125 being changed for a plug to one side matched by a decompressor on the other. The gearbox gained another speed and the 350 had a hand change with gate on the side of the tank in addition to the foot pedal, as required by the regulations.

The cycle parts were different from the 125, with the frame constructed from channel section steel pressings. The front forks continued to be blade girders and the frame to be rigid. A cantilever saddle was fitted and the rear carrier carried a bolt-on pillion seat plus grab handle for

DKW model NZ350 also built in 250 cc size. Both hand and foot gear levers were fitted

the services. It also supported full-sized pannier bags.

Much less common was the NZ500, which was used both solo and with a sidecar. Some were conscripts called to serve the Fatherland without the option, which meant that their riders had an interesting machine to sample.

The engine unit was a parallel twin with 64 × 76 mm dimensions for its slightly inclined cylinders. A single carburettor at the rear supplied both barrels and each had its own low-slung exhaust system. The four-speed gearbox was built in unit just as on the larger singles, and again both foot and hand gear controls were provided.

The cycle parts were generally as the NZ singles with the main exception of the addition of plunger rear suspension. The brakes were also larger, as were the tyre sections, but otherwise the standard of equipment was the same.

Postwar the factory at Zschopau became MZ, but the DKW name lived on and as always it only built two-strokes, and good ones at that.

NSU

To NSU surely falls the honour of producing the oddest 'motorcycle' of World War 2, although some would claim that the Kettenkraftrad was really a small, tracked, personnel carrier that just happened to have a motorcycle front fork. In truth it has to be admitted that a version without the front wheel was built as well and ran purely on its tracks.

NSU also made motorcycles in large numbers for the Wehrmacht in three sizes and all based on their prewar range. The smallest was a lightweight fitted with a 122 cc two-stroke single-cylinder engine built in unit with a three speed gearbox. Construction was conventional although twin exhausts and silencers were fitted as was the style of the period.

The 125 used a simple tubular cradle frame

with blade girder front forks and no rear suspension. The wheels were light with small drum brakes and 2.50 × 19 in. tyres. A cantilever saddle and rear carrier were fitted and the machine was a useful means of transporting one soldier over the shorter distances.

For harder work NSU provided the 251OS and 601OSL models, both with single-cylinder, pushrod ohv engines and separate four-speed gearboxes. The line was designed by Walter Moore, the Englishman who had been responsible for the first camshaft Norton, who had gone to Germany in 1929. As much of his Norton work was done in his own time he was able to take it with him and use it again. Thus both road and racing NSU models looked much as the early Norton ohv machines.

The lines of the two machines, of 241 and 562 cc, were thus English rather than German with fashionable twin port cylinder heads and both primary and final drives on the left. The 250 carried its oil in the crankcase in a compartment ahead of the flywheel chamber, but the 601 was a true dry sump model with separate oil tank under the saddle.

The 601 also had a full tubular cradle frame, unlike the 251, which made do with an open diamond, but both had girder forks, the lightweight with pressed steel blades and the other with tubes. Equipment was standard for the period with cantilever saddle, spoke wheels, drum brakes and full lighting. Both models had small pannier boxes either side of the rear wheel for tools. In the army these were changed for the usual full-sized bags and headlight masks were added.

The 251 was supplied to the Wehrmacht in quantity for some years, but in time was replaced by a DKW because, it was said, the DKW pulled the right strings in Berlin. A few 250s were sold to civilians during the war and after it some of the parts stock was used up by assembling machines to the War Office specification.

Like Victoria and Ardie, NSU built an aero-engine starter for the German air ministry and this used a flat twin air-cooled two-stroke that could run up to 10,000 rpm with peak torque between 6000 and 7000 rpm. This ran on petroil mixed at 20:1 and in use was run up to 10,000 rpm before the clutch was dropped to couple it to the aero engine. This pulled its speed down to the peak torque figure, which was just what was wanted to trundle a Junkers over until it fired up.

The tracked vehicle was more commonly known as a Kettenkrad and was powered by a 1478 cc ohv Opel four-cylinder, water-cooled engine. This drove a three-speed and reverse gearbox, which, coupled with a two-speed box, gave the driver the choice of six forward speeds in sets of high and low plus two reverse speeds.

The body ran on two tracks each with 40 rubber-faced links, with each joint in need of regular attention with a grease gun for the benefit of its needle races. The tracks ran round a total of six wheels on each side and steering was done with brakes on the front sprockets.

In front of the body was a motorcycle girder fork complete with a disc front wheel and a 3·50 × 19 in. tyre. At the top of the fork there was a headlight, a steering damper and a pair of handlebars complete with twistgrip. Movement of the bars caused the differential steering to operate and the role of the front wheel would seem to be rather limited as the vehicle was tracked.

The driver sat in the body with what were essentially car controls other than the handlebars and throttle. The body accommodated two rear-facing passengers at the back, but if needs be a good few more could perch on the structure somewhere. It was normal practice for the machine to tow a light trailer and in this form it would negotiate ditches, ford streams and cope with mud. Tow hitches enabled it to help other vehicles in difficulties and it could also tow a gun, or two, or a gun and its shells.

In fact it was a good all-round dogsbody for

getting other machines out of trouble and for hauling loads along. It served on most fronts and with most service branches as an all-purpose, general-haulage vehicle. So impressive was it that in 1945 a batch of 200 was ordered by the American Forestry Commission.

Right **A captured NSU being used by fitters while foraging spares from damaged vehicles**

NSU Kettenkrad on fire in the Egyptian desert during 1942

Military Motorcycles of World War 2

Far left **A line of captured Kettenkrads in the Western desert in 1944, long after El Alamein**

Below far left **A Kettenkrad on trial in England and demonstrating a little of its abilities**

Left **Kettenkrad controls with a combination of car and motorcycle practices. Note knee buffers for driver**

Below **Just after El Alamein and this NSU with trailers was used by these Axis troops to locate the British forces and surrender**

Germany – not just flat twins

115

No doubt they hauled logs well without turning a track. These, incidentally, could be changed by one man, who had to lay the new one in a line and then haul it over the rear wheel using a special hook. A good tool kit went under the rear seat to help with this and no doubt it was not too hard working on tarmac. In the desert it must have been a real *schweinhund*.

TWN

Triumph Werke Nürnberg was associated with the English Triumph company as early as 1903. In the early 1920s it was the English Junior two-

A TWN model BD250W ridden by a Maquis French resistance fighter with three GIs outside Brest

stroke model that they used to restart production and the links remained until 1929.

They continued with two-strokes in a range of conventional singles from 125 to 350 cc capacity and four-strokes with Swiss MAG proprietary engines, but for the army produced something a little special. This was the BD250W, which used a split single two-stroke engine with a geared rotary drum inlet valve. Some 12,000 were supplied to the Wehrmacht, in addition to a small batch of the standard 350S piston port single.

The two pistons of the 250 ran side by side in iron liners cast into the light alloy muff. Their job was not made any easier by the fitment of twin exhaust systems, one on each side. To keep the appearance neat and symmetrical the pipes came from the barrel corners, which meant a passage across the front of the block containing hot exhaust gases to connect both pipes to the one cylinder bore with exhaust ports.

The problem was not eased by the octane rating of the fuel used, which was a low 64, and the army's habit of running in a low gear for long periods. On army oil piston seizures were not unknown, although there was no trouble with civilian models, in both cases lubrication being by pump coupled to the throttle. Under army use the liners sometimes worked loose and it was intended to change to a one-piece cast iron barrel, but all the army machines had the alloy one.

The cylinder head with its single combustion chamber and 5·5:1 compression ratio was in light alloy. Each long piston was attached to its own rod, so the crankshaft was similar to that of a parallel twin. The big ends ran on needle rollers and the crankshaft with central flywheel on ball races.

Geared to the crankshaft and turning at the same speed was the inlet valve. This was a cylindrical drum whose axis lay behind and above the crankshaft. The drive gears lay at the left end of the two shafts and the carburettor went at the right end of the drum. Slots in the drum wall allowed the mixture into the cylinder.

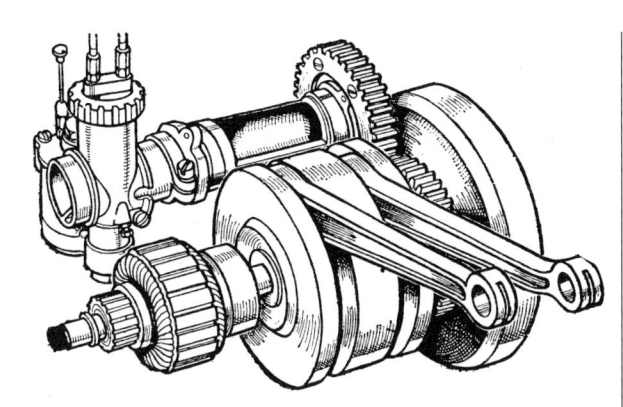

Crankshaft and rotary inlet valve of the TWN which had twin pistons and single combustion chamber

The four-speed gearbox was built in unit with the engine and with the carburettor enclosed also the unit looked very smooth and modern. Final drive was by chain on the right, fully enclosed and with a cast alloy cover over the rear sprocket and flexible tubes for each chain run.

The frame was rigid and constructed from tubes and pressings in steel. The front forks were blade girders with a single central compression spring. Rider comfort was looked after by a cantilever saddle. Both wheels had 3·25 × 19 in. tyres and both were slowed by 150 mm single leading shoe drum brakes.

The oil tank for the pump system went under the saddle and the horn hung beneath the fuel tank behind the engine. The toolbox went on top of the fuel tank for the army and the contents enabled the rider to adjust the rubber suspension of the saddle to suit his weight and the footrests to suit his leg length.

Panniers were fitted either side of the rear carrier, but little else was needed to make the TWN a very nice machine for army use. On test it was able to reach 65 mph carrying a passenger, handled well and had good brakes. In service use it was generally reliable.

In addition to the BD250W the firm were involved in the design of other motorcycle items.

One was an engine for the NSU tracked machine and was an extension of the split single, twin piston idea. The design called for a total of eight pistons arranged in a vee formation to give four combustion chambers. In turn this design led to a split single based on one-quarter of the vee eight, but neither went beyond the drawing board.

Another project never to get beyond the prototype stage was an airborne scooter that had to knock down for minimum shipping size. Its specification called for 125 cc, a three-speed gearbox, 30 mph speed, 132 lb weight and the ability to carry a 330 lb load some 180 miles. Tyre size was to be 400 × 7 in. and the resulting machine thus had split rims in pressed steel.

The machine had a conventional single-cylinder, two-stroke engine built in unit with the gearbox. The cylinder was inclined forward and the carburettor tucked in behind it, while the exhaust ran down and under the unit.

The frame was built up from one large pressing and a number of tubes. The main tube ran back and down from the headstock area as a down tube, which went beneath the engine. At its rear end was attached a further tube shaped into a U and this continued the line either side of the rear wheel.

Above the engine went the pressing in the form of a large flat sheet, perforated with slots and flanged down at the edges. It ran back from the front end of the down tube to the rear wheel, where it was braced by struts. Under it went a long thin fuel tank and this, and the rear wheel, were enclosed by a panel.

At the front end went a detachable steering head and front fork. From the head a tube ran back and was clamped into the down tube so it could be quickly assembled. In the head was fitted the steering column with short telescopic forks and quickly released bars.

The seat was supported on two pillars so could be demounted with ease, while the footrests folded up. When apart the pieces tucked into a small box; assembly only taking a few moments.

It could have been useful, but was not to be so TWN continued to build their 250 split single.

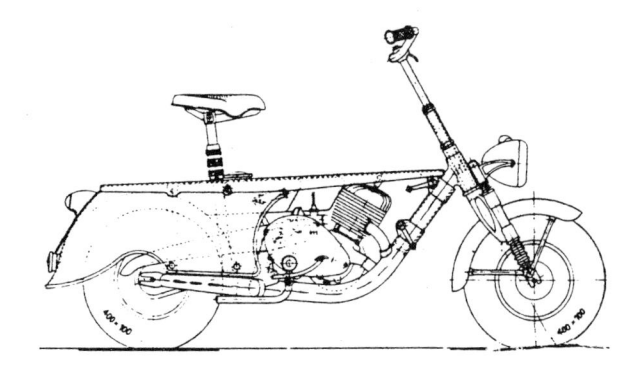

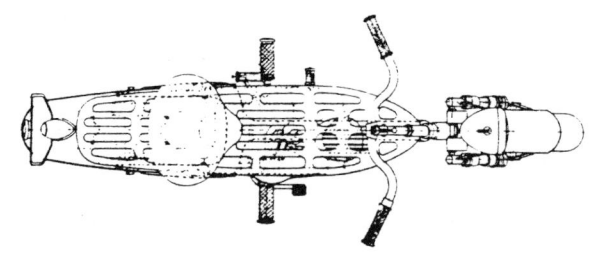

The TWN airborne scooter prototype which reduced to parts for packing

Victoria

This company was founded in Victorian times to make bicycles and they continued in that field for long after they added motorcycles to their lists. Powered machines came just before the turn of the century, so the firm had a long history within the German industry.

During the war period they concentrated on a four-stroke single, their KR35WH, which had been sold prewar as a light sports model. The 342 cc engine was a long-stroke with dimensions of 69 × 91·5 mm and ran on a 6·0 : 1 compression ratio. It was built in unit with the four-speed gearbox and as the pushrods for the overhead valves were enclosed in a single tube it had the appearance of a camshaft motor.

The timing case, on the right, looked much as the NSU but merely enclosed a gear pair and the drive for the plunger oil pump. Lubrication was wet sump with the same oil looking after engine and transmission. The valve gear was fully enclosed and the generator was mounted on the left end of the crankshaft, so a very clean unit resulted. A two-port head was fitted so twin exhaust systems were used, one each side. The engine was brought in from Columbus, the proprietary engine division of the Horex motorcycle company.

The power unit went into a frame of the open diamond type with a substantial pressed steel down tube. The seat member and rear frame were tubes and there was no rear suspension. The front forks were pressed steel blade girders with a single central compression spring and both brakes were single leading shoe drum.

Equipment was comprehensive, with the rear chain fully enclosed and a toolbox set in the top of the fuel tank. The saddle sat on two coil springs and a pillion seat with grab handle could be mounted on the rear carrier as an assembly. Panniers were fitted on each side and their use meant that the exhaust systems had to be modified. On the civilian model they were upswept with high-level silencers, but for the army the pipes ran at crankcase-top level and then swept down to the silencers. Together with the DKW 125 and 350, the KR35WH was produced until the very end of the war.

In addition to the 350 there were other Victoria models used in the war, but these were conscripted from civilian ranks and modified for service use. One such was the KR25, which had a 250 cc single-cylinder, two-stroke engine with twin exhausts built in unit with a four-speed gearbox.

Engine construction was conventional and the cycle parts as for the 350 in general layout and design. For the army the high exhausts were swept low, a toolbox was set on the tank top and panniers fitted.

Useful machines for the Wehrmacht.

Zundapp

All-chain gearboxes, four-valve heads, an opposed piston two-stroke, a shaft-drive single and the green elephant model all indicate how Zundapp have been at the forefront of technical innovation since their foundation in 1917. Over the years they built machines of all sizes and types up to a one-litre, supercharged flat four for world record attempts.

The company's reputation is founded on the reliability of their models, which is exceptional, together with the unusual engineering of many features. In many areas the observer is left with the impression that the models were designed by an engineer of the highest ability who was recruited from another field and thus lacked motorcycle experience. The result was a series of machines that proved to be very well engineered, very reliable and to have their own special feel to the rider. Very effective.

Many of their models were flat twins and the bulk of those supplied to the services were of that type. In addition they continued to build the very popular DB200, which with minor additions proved most helpful to the Wehrmacht.

The DB200 was a perfectly conventional single-cylinder two-stroke with a vertical barrel in iron and an alloy head. The carburettor went at the rear and it had twin exhaust ports connected to two separate silencing systems mounted low down. The crankcase split vertically and also carried the three-speed gearbox to give unit construction and at first sight the machine had an engine-mounted clutch. In fact the bulge in the primary drive case on the right concealed a flywheel and the clutch went with the gearbox and was driven by chain.

Final drive was on the left, so the gearbox was

119

of the cross-over design and its ratios were selected by a hand lever working in a small gate on the right side of the fuel tank and disguised as a kneegrip. The complete engine unit went into a rigid frame built up from pressings and tubes. The main member comprised the headstock with top and tank rails and to this was bolted the rest, with downtube and rear subframe, all tubular and all held together by bolts, and the engine unit.

The front forks were blade girders and the wheels were shod with 3·00 × 19 in. tyres. Equipment included a battery tucked in behind the engine unit low down on the right, a centre

Left **Captured Zundapp two-stroke in France**

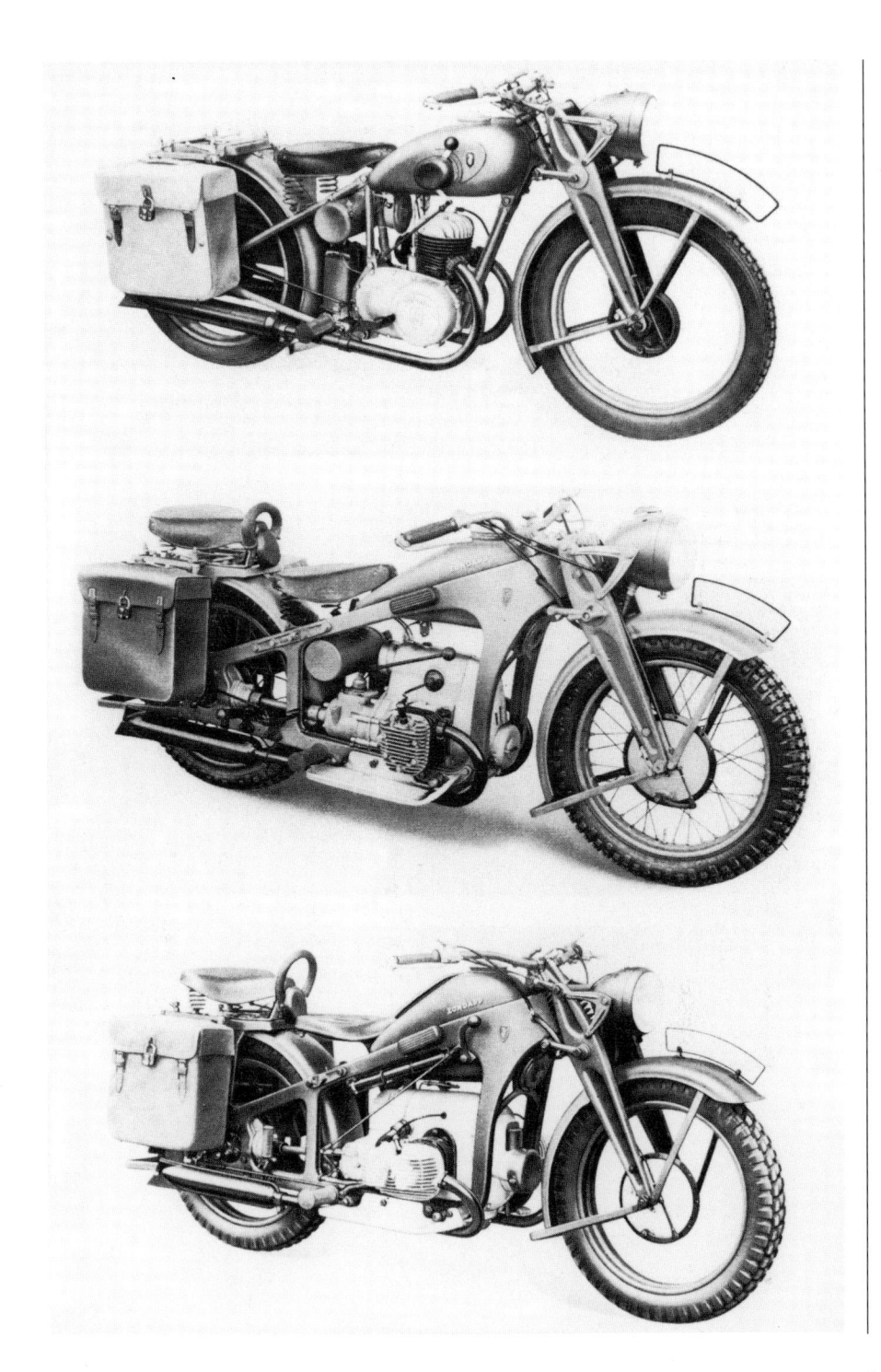

Right top **Zundapp DB200W**, a conventional two-stroke for general duties

Right centre **K500W** flat twin with side valve engine in pressed steel frame

Right **KS600W** with overhead valve engine and other variations from the smaller flat twin

Germany – not just flat twins

stand, a cylindrical toolbox under the saddle and for the army the inevitable panniers. No pillion seat was fitted to the rear carrier but provision was made for one.

All the other machines supplied were multis and the older pair had side valves. The smaller was the K500 flat twin, which had an oversquare engine, a modest compression ratio and a similar power output. The design dated back to 1933 and was typical of Zundapp flat twin engines. The crankshaft was a single forging, but rather than use white metal bearings the German firm favoured needle rollers in the split big end with cap screws to hold the two parts of the rod together.

The crankcase was cast in the barrel form with the crankshaft inserted from the rear. Due to the

Zundapp sidecar outfits on exercise

The K800W flat four Zundapp seen here captured and obeying a company sergeant major in 1944

A K800W with typical Wehrmacht sidecar with tonneau and fabric side door

sizes of the parts it was necessary to assemble the crankshaft into the crankcase and then to fit the connecting rods with their split needle cages. This was done through the cylinder holes in the sides of the case and was not the easiest of jobs. Once complete, the pistons were added and then the cylinders and their heads.

Under the crankcase went a ribbed sump and the case front formed the back of the timing chest. In this a gear pair drove down to the oil pump of the wet sump system and a chain drove up to the camshaft. An outer cover completed the timing chest and the generator was fixed to the crankshaft nose ahead of this under a further lid. The valve gear was completed by tappets whose adjusters were accessible on removal of a small plate on the upper side of each cylinder.

The ignition coils were set in the top of the crankcase casting with short leads out to the plugs. A top cover enclosed the coils and extended to the rear of the engine to also encompass the carburettor. This had a visible air filter and fed a tract that ran down in the crankcase, split into two and ran out through each cylinder to the inlet port. Each exhaust had a pipe that ran forward from the cylinder and then back to a low-level silencer.

The clutch and gearbox were bolted to the rear of the engine to produce a single smoothly contoured unit and from the rear of this came the shaft drive. This went on the right; the shaft itself was exposed, with joints at each end to accommodate minor alignment variations.

The gearbox was the famous four-speed, all-chain type with pre-stretched duplex roller chains connecting the two shafts. Dog clutches engaged the sprockets under the guidance of selectors and these hung into the box from above. A car-type hand lever and ball gate moved the selectors and the control was by the right hand.

The kickstart lever had a folding pedal and went on the left. Its shaft was attached to a bevel gear and from this a spur pair stepped the drive into the gearbox mainshaft. Both gear pairs were enclosed in a further small casting and cover which bolted to that of the gearbox.

The power unit went into a frame built up from channel section pressed steel welded together.

Germany – not just flat twins

123

The Zundapp KS750 mit Beiwagen. A wide angle V-twin engine, many gears and gear levers and sidecar wheel drive

One Captain 'Hippo' Hensman with a KS750 late in 1944. The ribbed box alongside the rear wheel is the silencer

The frame was fully duplex, with the fuel tank set between the upper members, and was rigid with blade girder front forks. Good-sized drum brakes went into the wire-spoked wheels, which were shod with 3·50 × 19 in. tyres. Equipment was comprehensive and included panniers and pillion seat with grab handle, while for times of need a cylindrical toolbox was fitted across the frame beneath the saddle. Footboards and footrests were provided for the rider.

A little younger was the overhead-valve KS600. It was also larger thanks to a small increase in stroke and bigger one in the bore and on the surface looked much as the 500. Beneath the covers there were changes with gear drive to the camshaft in addition to the necessary alterations to the valve gear and cylinder heads.

These had rockers pivoting on shafts held to bearing pads and neat covers with fins to match the cylinder head.

The ignition coils were completely enclosed under the top cover along with the carburettor, which supplied its mixture via trunking to the head on each side. The cover extended back over the gearbox and the change mechanism was altered to provide a foot pedal on the left, while on the right went a linkage rod from the selectors up to a hand lever on the frame beside the fuel tank.

The longer cover also meant that the toolbox had to move, a space being provided for it under a lid in the tank top. In addition a tyre pump appeared on the right top frame member. The saddle type changed from rear springs to cantilever, but in most other respects the 600 copied the 500 in layout and equipment.

The second, older, side-valve model was the K800 and this had a flat four engine built on the same lines as the twins. Again there were changes under the covers, but in appearance they all looked very similar and construction followed the same basic methods.

The timing chest used the gear drive to the oil pump with a chain drive up to the camshaft. For ignition a distributor was used and this, with its contact points, was mounted as an assembly on front of the timing chest. In that position it was skew gear driven from the nose of the crankshaft. The coil was mounted alongside it. A single cover enclosed the whole works and the ignition leads ran back internally to emerge two on each side for the plugs.

The front end of the camshaft carried a spur gear, which drove a dynamo mounted on top of the crankcase under a cover. This extended back to enclose the single carburettor and as on the K500 the inlet passages ran internally through crankcase and blocks to the valves.

An exhaust pipe emerged from front and rear of each block and ran to the rear, where both fed into a low-slung common silencer on each side. The rear pipe was shielded by a ribbed pressing that fitted round the back of the cylinder head and ran back to just behind the footrest. As with the other models, footboards were also supplied.

Above **Same KS750 with the engine unit removed to show frame construction and the fork legs made in a similar welded fashion**

Top **Zundapp under investigation in 1945. This shows the clean lines of the frame and the girder fork links**

Germany – not just flat twins

125

The transmission of the 800 was as for the 500 with hand change on the right and shaft drive. The cycle parts were also the same as far as frame, forks, wheels, tanks and toolbox were concerned, but the cantilevered saddle was fitted.

The 800 was frequently fitted with a sidecar but was also used as a solo, while the 600 was used in either form. Neither had sidecar wheel drive and their tyre section was too narrow to cope with Flanders mud, which led in time to the very special sidecar outfits developed for the Wehrmacht by both BMW and Zundapp.

The latter received an order from the War Office late in November 1939 to build two prototypes with sidecar wheel drive and to carry out tests on them. These were required for completion by the end of March 1940 and then a further order brought finalization tests. A month earlier a separate order called for a batch of five and another batch of 15 machines – the KS750 was off and running. Mass production, however, did not start before the end of 1941.

The new machine employed many of the well-known Zundapp features but also differed in many areas. The first was that the engine was not a flat twin but a vee with the very wide angle of 170 degrees. Thus each cylinder was tilted up a little from the horizontal. It was capped by an alloy head with valve inserts, which with a flat top piston gave a 6·2 : 1 compression ratio.

The engine still used needle roller big ends and a crankcase in which the crankshaft was assembled from the rear. It ran in one roller and one ball bearing with helical gears at the front, driving up to the camshaft and down to the oil pump. From the camshaft a spur gear pair drove the magneto, mounted on top of the crankcase and enclosed under a cover with the single carburettor. As on the 600 the mixture was fed through casting and hose to the inlet port.

The exhaust system was different. The two pipes connected to a chamber set across the frame ahead of the crankcase sump and from

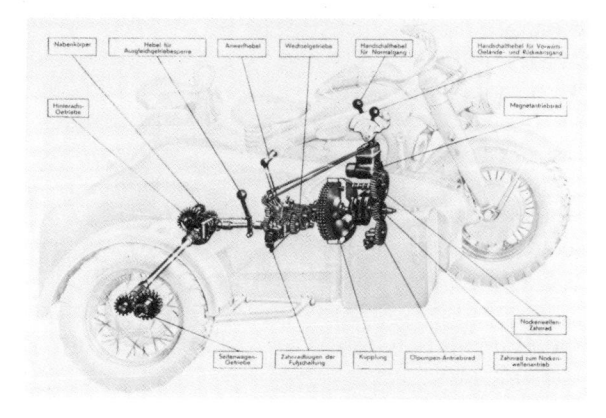

Zundapp KS750 gears and controls to connect crankshaft to magneto, oil pump, camshaft and wheels

this a single pipe ran to the rear on the left. It connected to a silencer box, set between the chinstays, which was ribbed and looked like a toolbox but just dealt with the exhaust gases.

The transmission was a little complex and all done with gear wheels. A two-speed box behind the clutch gave the choice of high or low ratios and drove into the main four-speed gearbox. Coupled into the train was a box to give forward or reverse gears and from this collection a shaft drove back to the rear wheel. Control of the boxes was by left foot for the four speeds and by two hand levers on the right for the others. The inboard one selected high or low and the outer the machine direction of travel.

There were more gears at the rear end, starting with a crown wheel and pinion. This drove a differential that split the torque in proportion to the needs. It could also be locked solid by use of a lever under the saddle behind the engine unit. From the differential a spur gear pair in the bevel box took the drive back to the rear wheel, which was quickly detachable. It was also interchangeable with the other two.

The differential unit also drove a shaft that ran across the sidecar chassis to the wheel hub assembly, where a further gear pair carried the drive forward to the wheel itself and by the use of the two sets of gears the sidecar lead was set. Both rear and sidecar wheels were hydraulically braked using a single foot pedal, while the front used a lever system to work the two shoes without a cam and was the same as the BMW.

The KS750 frame was built up from pressings welded together to form oval-section tubes. These ran from headstock to rear spindle to form a fully duplex cradle frame with two cross-members. It was expensive to make due to the amount of welding, but was light and strong. The sidecar chassis was built in a similar fashion, with the wheel drive enclosed and the wheel on a leading arm with torsion tube springing. The body was sprung on torsion bars.

The Zundapp front forks looked like heavy-duty telescopics constructed from oval tubing. They were actually girders with the main members formed as pressings welded together. The fork springs went inside the legs and were loaded by rocker arms at the tops. Hydraulic damping was included in the mechanism, which was fully enclosed and less liable to damage in the field than the BMW telescopic fork. For this reason it was scheduled to be used by both makes in later orders, but it was a very complicated affair to set up and service, so BMW continued using their own telescopic fork.

For the rest the Zundapp was as the BMW with rugged construction for military use. As usual for the former marque the fuel tank sat between the frame members. Full equipment was fitted; the toolbox fitting into the tank top. The rider had a sprung saddle, a pillion seat and grab handle assembly went on top of the rear carrier and a pannier hung on the left side. No footboards were fitted, only rests, and controls were conventional.

The sidecar was as for the BMW with spare wheel on the rear deck and fittings on the nose for panniers, jerricans, radio or weapons. A *tonneau* and fabric side door were available and the chair wheel was protected by a chassis tube ahead of it as well as by its mudguard.

Like the BMW it was a very sophisticated piece of machinery, and with it was superseded by the simple 350 cc DKW single in 1944.

8 Italy – war stopped the racing

It is impossible to believe that the Italian people had any real interest in the war. To most it was simply an interruption to the essentials of life – women, Chianti and racing. The world may have gone mad but that was no reason not to follow the fortunes of Alfa Romeo and Maserati, Gilera and Guzzi.

So in 1940 they ran the Mille Miglia, Tripoli Grand Prix and Targa Florio for cars and Milano-Taranto, Modena and finally Genoa for motorcycles. That final event drew an interesting 500 cc grid with the blown Guzzi triple on the front row with the blown Gilera. No sooner was the fighting over than a race meeting was being run, even if the conditions were primitive. The course was short, machines few, crowd control minimal and enthusiasm high.

For the Italians the war was over and they could return to important matters.

Benelli

Benelli hit the headlines in 1939 with a win in the 250 cc TT and some of the military machines reflected this with their ohc engines. These came in 250 and 500 cc single forms and were both built along similar lines. Dimensions were 67 × 70 mm and 85 × 87 mm to give 247 and 494 cc capacities. In both cases the camshaft drive was on the right with the points for the coil ignition and the rocking pedal for the four-

250 cc Benelli single, a typical Italian design with overhead camshaft engine and pivoted rear fork suspension

128

One of the real Italian interests, road racing, and the start line at Genoa in May 1940 with Serafini on the blown Gilera (6) and Sandri on the blown Guzzi triple (2)

speed gearbox.

Although both engines had an overhead camshaft the 250 had hairpin valve springs, but the 500 was fitted with duplex coil springs. Both were exposed and on the 250 the springs were soft enough to be changed by hand. The engines had twin port heads and each exhaust system had a lever to put its baffle out of action, so the Italian rider could choose his noise level.

The lubricating oil was carried in a ribbed forward extension of the crankcase and on top of this went a tiny oil cooler set between the duplex downtubes. The dynamo was clamped into the crankcase, but driven via a rubber coupling, and could be removed by taking out one screw.

The frame was tubular, with girder forks at the front controlled by a single compression spring. At the rear went a pivoted fork linked to plungers built into the end of the frame and further controlled by friction lever dampers. Drum brakes, lighting equipment and army equipment completed the package.

Benelli also made a tricycle in typical Italian fashion by adding a platform body on a two-wheeled axle behind a conventional motorcycle.

These were fitted with the 500 cc engine with a lengthy chain drive to the rear and were used by the Italians in various forms to carry men, stores or the heavier form of machine gun.

Very handy in times of stress.

Bianchi

The racing Bianchi of 1939 was a transverse 500 cc four with shaft-driven overhead camshaft, but the military models were less exciting. They only had one cylinder and relied on side valves to inhale and exhaust their mixture.

For those that deserved them they also built a model with an overhead camshaft and more go. Both machines were 500s and of fairly conventional design. Typical of the Italian industry of the period was the use of rear suspension with a swinging fork for the wheel controlled by springs in plunger boxes and friction lever dampers.

Not as exciting as a four but better for the army.

Gilera

In the competition world Gilera was well known in the late 1930s for its very successful blown racing four and the world's one-hour record a fully streamlined version had taken. For the Italian army the machines were very prosaic side-valve models and thus they were just as Norton, who raced the Manx but sold the 16H to the military.

The model from 1936 to 1944 was the LTE and based on a civilian one. Its engine was a simple side valve of near vintage design using the traditional Gilera dimensions of 84 × 90 mm, which gave a capacity of 499 cc. A very modest 4·5 : 1 compression ratio enabled it to produce 10 bhp at 3400 rpm, all figures below the civil machine.

The engine had a built-up crankshaft with roller big end and ball bearing mains. The piston was flat topped and ran in an iron barrel capped by a head with vertical fins cast in the same material. The valves were fully enclosed with an access cover on the side of the cylinder and were opened by cams, cam followers and tappets all on the right. The camshaft was gear driven from the crankshaft and ran just above it. From the cam gear an idler drove the magneto, which sat ahead of the cylinder. The dynamo went beneath it in front of the crankcase.

Lubrication was by wet sump and the oil pump was driven from the crankshaft via a vertical shaft. The sump extended forward beneath the electrics and back under the gearbox for the full width of the engine and incorporated a filler and a breather.

The primary transmission was by duplex chain on the left, and this and the multi-plate clutch were enclosed by a cast light alloy case. The gearbox bolted on to a platform formed as part of the crankcase casting, so the assembly fitted together as a semi-unit construction. The gearbox was conventional, with four speeds selected by a hand lever attached to the right side of the tank, final drive by chain on the left and the kick-start pedal on the right.

The frame was tubular and incorporated the Gilera form of rear suspension with control by springs set in horizontal tubes either side of the rear wheel at carburettor level. Each side of the rear fork was a triangle of tubes with an apex at the rear wheel spindle. At a glance the construction was much as the chainstays of a rigid frame, but closer inspection showed the fork pivot halfway up the vertical triangle side. At the top of this member the triangle was linked by rod to the spring boxes, with friction lever dampers on each side of the machine.

The pillion footrests were hung from the spring boxes when the machine was built to carry a passenger, and in this case a pair of bars was provided for him to cling to. These folded back when not in use and this movement was linked to the spring boxes to vary the spring rate.

Front suspension was by girder forks with a compression spring to take the load and friction dampers to control it. The wheels had single leading shoe drum brakes and the rear was heel operated by the left foot. The ends of the footrests were braced to the front of the engine with stays that swept obstacles to the side. An air filter was fitted and the exhaust pipe swept down on the right and then ran in serpentine manner to the cylindrical silencer with fishtail. A saddle, toolboxes of two types, depending on whether the machine was built for a passenger, lights, horn and a sturdy centre stand completed the picture.

The LTE was used solo or with a sidecar, which was normally seen fitted on the left – English – side. Two chassis types were used, both with a sprung wheel, and two body styles. A third chassis with rigid wheel and single-seat body with rear-mounted spare wheel was also used.

The military sidecar body was a more functional device with no door, open body and crude fittings. A screen was provided along with plenty of hand holds, so the passenger could play his part in keeping the outfit stable.

On a more serious level Gilera also produced the Marte model, which came with a sidecar in its military form. This machine was much as the LTE with a 499 cc side valve engine but with a light alloy cylinder head, 5:1 compression ratio and increased power output of 14 bhp at 4800 rpm.

Most of the engine details were the same, but, apart from having four speeds, the transmission was very different. The first change was that primary drive was by gears. The gearchange continued to be by hand, but the drive was then taken via a pair of bevel gears to a shaft to drive the rear wheel. The rear bevel box drove the rear wheel from the crown wheel and included a spur gear pair that drove a cross-shaft ahead of the rear axle. A second spur gear pair at the sidecar wheel took the drive back again so the two rear

The Gilera LTE, a machine with side valve engine and pivoted fork rear suspension built 1936–44

wheels were in line. The sidecar gears also included a dog clutch controlled by a hand lever on the machine to engage the drive as required.

The frame was much as the LTE, but the rear fork was modified on the right side to become a bellcrank constructed from steel pressings welded together. The suspension medium remained the same and the front forks were still girders. The sidecar wheel continued to be on a trailing arm and in this case the sidecar went on the right of the machine so that the drive matched to the chair.

It would therefore seem that Gilera alone solved the problem of allowing the rear wheel to have a suspension system while driving the

Late 1940 Western desert photograph of a captured Gilera LTE

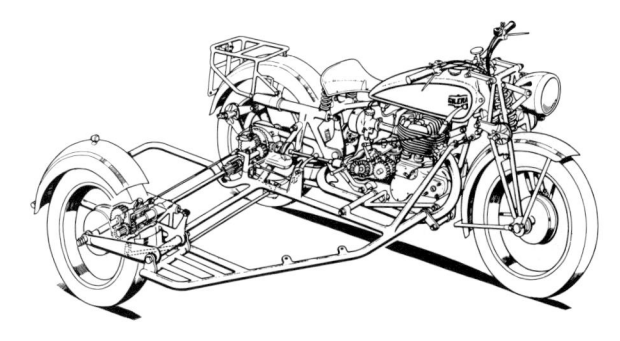

The Gilera Marte much as the LTE but the sidecar wheel drive added without the loss of rear suspension. Shaft drive to rear wheel

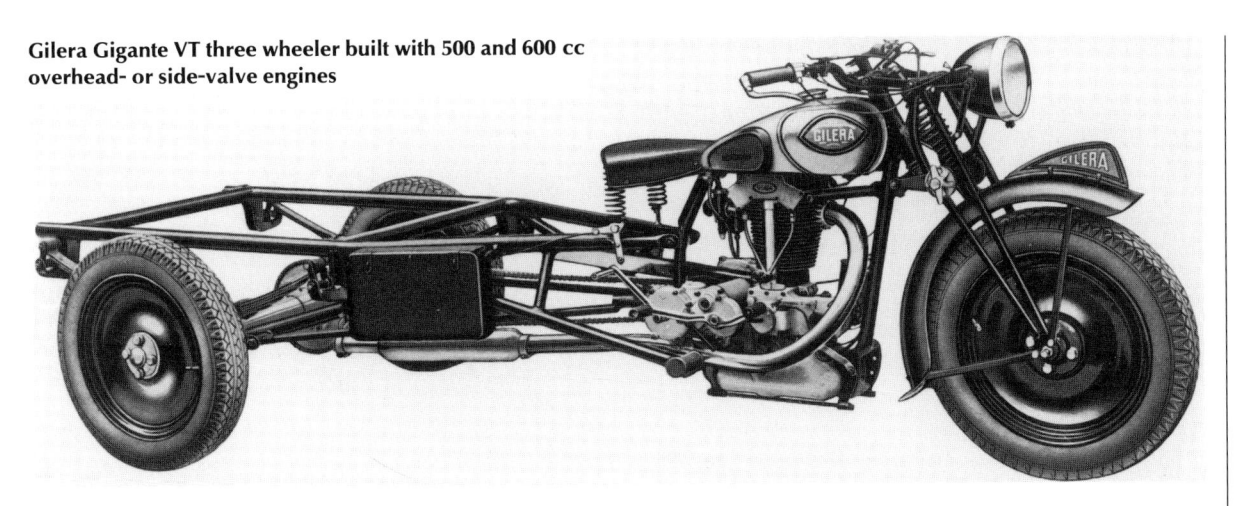

Gilera Gigante VT three wheeler built with 500 and 600 cc overhead- or side-valve engines

sidecar wheel. Norton, BMW, Zundapp, Gnome et Rhone and the Belgian firms all kept to rigid rear wheels even if the chair one moved.

The sidecar body was military and functional with a single seat, a folding screen and a spare wheel on the rear panel. Its wheel was braked and it was able to mount a machine gun for use on the move.

Gilera also built three-wheeled load carriers based on a motorcycle back to the saddle plus a rear axle and load-carrying chassis. On this all types of body were possible to carry stores or a gun. The engine was the side-valve unit in either 500 or 600 cc forms or a 500 cc ohv unit, and in all cases built on normal Gilera lines.

In 1940 these models were joined by the Mercurio and this used the ohv engine in 500 cc form, which postwar had its stroke lengthened to make it a 600. The engine construction followed normal Gilera practice but the unit was

The Marte in solo form, typical of Gilera models except for the shaft drive

Italy – war stopped the racing

133

turned so the crankshaft lay along the machine. It was thus able to directly drive the clutch and this in turn the four-speed gearbox with its hand change. From this a propeller shaft ran to the rear axle suspended on semi-elliptic springs.

The frame was new, its main member being a massive tube that ran back from the headstock, under the saddle to the rear platform frame. A pair of loops hung from it to support the engine and gearbox unit and the front forks were blade girders. Wheels were smaller in diameter with heavier-section tyres and all three had drum brakes.

All manner of equipment could be carried by these vehicles and they proved most useful to the services during the war.

Moto Guzzi

Since 1921 Mandello del Lario have produced many of the world's most original motorcycles, always Italian in style but with their own unique blend of engineering function unlike anything else. Often ugly in that controls, cables, pipes

Moto Guzzi GT17 with passenger grips, footrests and rear suspension preload linked together

and parts run in anything but a stylish line, but at the same time beautiful in the efficient use of metal and energy.

The most traditional Guzzi engine style is the horizontal single, with its massive outside flywheel on the left, magneto on top of the crankcase and gearbox built-in unit and sharing the same oil as the engine.

The GT17 was in this form, and during the 1930s was a stable diet for the Italian army. It

Moto Guzzi Alce derived from GT20 and carrying a heavy machine gun

was so very typical of the marque, even its engine dimensions of 88 × 82 mm were those of the first Guzzi machine. They gave a capacity of 499 cc and on a compression ratio of 4·7 :1 the engine produced 13·2 bhp at 4000 rpm.

Engine construction was as the 1921 motor with iron head and barrel with longitudinal fins. The camshaft was above the crankshaft, gear driven, and in turn drove the magneto. The inlet side had a side valve opened directly by a cam follower and tappet, but the exhaust was overhead and held shut by a single hairpin spring. It was opened by a bellcrank cam follower, tappet, pushrod and external rocker.

Lubrication was by dry sump with the oil pumps driven by the crankshaft and positioned low down in the crankcase. The carburettor was a Dell'Orto with separate float chamber and the instrument faced to the left. A manifold carried the mixture to the engine. The exhaust pipe came from beneath the engine to run back to a silencer on the left. This comprised two cylindrical bodies, one above the other, and a fishtail outlet.

Primary drive was by a pair of gears on the left to a multi-plate clutch. This drove a three-speed gearbox in which the ratios were hand selected by a lever working in a gate on the right side of the tank. The box was of the cross-over design so the final drive chain was on the right, as were the clutch arm and the kickstart pedal. The dynamo was strapped to the top of the crankcase and gearbox casting aft of the magneto and was driven by the clutch primary gear.

Moto Guzzi were among the earliest of firms that believed in suspension for both wheels so the GT17 had a sprung rear wheel. The main frame, by contrast, was nearly conventional with top tube and wide splayed twin downtubes. The seat member was not a tube but plates that supported the rear fork and extended below the pivot point. Beneath the engine unit went a further pressed steel assembly and this contained

An Alce under examination in England and lacking a few parts

the suspension springs. Rods linked them to the rear fork, which was made as a braced bellcrank to carry the loads.

Damping was by friction lever units mounted either side between the end of the fork and the rear subframe, which bolted to the main one. Further ingenuity enabled the spring rate to be increased when a pillion passenger was carried. This person was provided with a seat supported from the main and subframes and sat at a level above the rider. He was also provided with a pair of handlebars, which could fold back and down to the horizontal, plus footrests on arms that hung down in use and swung back when not. Bars and rests were linked and a further rod coupled their movement to the rear suspension so that as the bars were raised so was the spring rate.

The rider could also use the mechanism to stiffen the suspension over rough country, but at the front he had to manage with ordinary girder forks with a single compression spring, a pair of tension rebound springs and friction dampers. The wheels were conventional with wire spokes, single leading shoe drum brakes and 3·50 × 19 in. tyres. The rear was worked by a pedal on the left that connected to the cam lever by a two-piece rod to ensure that wheel movement did not affect brake operation. The pedal was pivoted at a point beneath the rider's foot and pointed back, with the pad almost in line with the flywheel centre, where it was intended to be pressed by the rider's heel.

A good roll-on centre stand was fitted and the fuel tank had a toolbox set in it. The oil tank went across the frame beneath the front of the fuel

Moto Guzzi Alce with sidecar, motocarrozzetta, 1940 model

The Trialce with rear axle and supporting a heavy machine gun

tank and just behind it on the right was the horn. The rider had footboards for his feet and attached to them were legshields, which run up to the base of the tank. A headlamp was clipped to the front forks to complete the basic machine.

For the army it could come with extras and one such was a sub-machine gun mounted in front of the rider, the theory being that he could ride into battle spraying the area ahead with bullets. It would seem that the army came to the conclusion that this was not too clever an idea to put in volatile Italian hands.

The model was also fitted out to carry a heavy machine gun and its tripod, which would seem to have been safer for all parties. In this guise it lost a pair of small boxes supplied when the sub-machine gun was fitted and most likely used for ammunition.

The GT17 was built from 1932 to 1939 and was then superseded for the war years by the Alce. This was derived from the GT20 of 1938 and overall the changes were minimal. An extra ratio went into the gearbox and a positive stop mechanism appeared on top of the casting but remained linked to a lever on the right of the fuel tank. From the mechanism a cable went to an indicator on top of the tank to tell the rider which gear he was in.

The carburettor gained an air filter and the exhaust pipe fed into a pair of silencers mounted one above the other, with a guard over the top of the flywheel, but otherwise the engine was little altered and remained typical Guzzi.

The frame was modified but stayed on earlier lines, except that the rear spring variation was deleted. The subframe and fittings altered but real changes were few. One was to move the rear brake drum to the right side with the sprocket and to change its operating pedal, although this remained under the heel.

The Alce could be fitted to carry a passenger or a gun and tripod as before but had additional variations, for example, an adaptation with skis was built as an experiment for use in the Alps,

and several sidecars. These were fitted on either side of the machine and were all single seaters with sprung wheel, limited protection, no door and the spare wheel hung on the rear panel.

A further version built around 1942 was fitted with smaller wheel rims and much fatter section tyres. The rear wheel went on a stub axle and was suspended on a true swinging arm without a left fork leg. This model also used the GT17 oil tank.

A variation on three wheels was the Trialce, which was based on the carrier vehicles the firm had built since 1928. From the front wheel to the saddle the machine was stock Guzzi, but the rear was extended to a two-wheeled axle and a load-carrying platform. Various bodies were built on this to carry goods or stores and for the army it could be easily adapted as a mobile heavy machine gun complete with shield to protect the user. A very efficient way of moving fire power about at speed.

A variation on this theme was the Motocarri, which was built on heavier lines and used the ohv engine with a three-speed gearbox. This drove a rear axle suspended on semi-elliptic springs. Behind the rider went a platform body that could be open or hooded and was able to support a much heavier gun firing cannon shells.

The machine form dated from 1928 and was built in many sizes before and after the war. In later years some managed with a mere 50 cc, but as early as 1934 one was built with a 238 cc engine. Postwar, one was fitted with an unusual engine for a Guzzi, not only was it a flat twin but it was also a diesel.

Yet another unusual method of moving and using fire power was based on the more sporting GTS model. This was a GT17 with the four-speed gearbox and less weight. It could be fitted with a sub-machine gun in its simpler style, but was also fitted out to work as an armoured machine gun point.

In this form it carried the machine gun as usual with a shield on the handlebars. A guard swung

Italy – war stopped the racing

down to protect the front tyre and in use the saddle swung up so the rider sat much lower on the frame and behind the shield. With the machine on its centre stand and his feet up on the footrests behind the legshields the rider was well tucked out of harm's way.

After the war in 1946 the Alce became the Superalce, with overhead valves, footchange and a little more power. Otherwise there was little change until 1950, when the military Falcone appeared with telescopic forks.

In addition to the 500 cc machines used by the Italian army they also had a number of similar 250s. These were the Airone model and were built very much as the GT17 and Alce machines. The 246 cc capacity came from 70 × 64 mm

Italian police on Moto Guzzis meeting a convoy of Kings African Rifles who led the way into Addis Ababa in April 1941

dimensions and the engine had overhead valves. The remainder was as the 500 with four-speed gearbox, magneto ignition, girder forks and swinging fork frame. Different was the left kick-starter and usual the left rear brake drum, rear-facing pedal, oil tank beneath the front of the fuel tank and the outside flywheel. The single silencer went on the right and postwar it was fitted with telescopic forks.

Strangest of all was the Autoveicolo da montagna, or Mulo Meccanico as it became known. Mechanical Mule was a good name for this all-purpose three-wheeler, which was driven by a transverse ohv V-twin of 754 cc. In later years the power unit sired a whole series of motorcycles.

The Mule appeared in 1960 and was built solely for the army, who wanted a cross-country vehicle that could cope with just about anything.

138

Moto Guzzi GTS corazzata (ironclad), a neat way of providing a firing platform, protecting the gunner and keeping it mobile

The resultant layout was as the Trialce but on a much larger and heavier scale. Thus the tyres were 6·00 × 15 in. and the single front wheel was carried by a single massive, telescopic strut on the left.

Steering was by a wheel and the front end was further complicated because the road wheel was driven by a whole series of shafts and gears. One-fifth of the available power was split off by the differential for this purpose. The rest went to the twin rear wheels, each of which was separately driven by a shaft running down the wheel arm to a crown wheel and pinion.

Each rear wheel assembly had a small disc wheel carried behind it on an arm. Normally these were clear of the ground, but for extra

Early experimental Guzzi driven by 500 cc single engine and fitted with full armour

traction they would be swung down and a caterpillar track fitted round them and the main wheels. They gave the machine extraordinary climbing ability.

The engine power went through a six-speed and reverse gearbox and the mechanics went into a sturdy chassis built to carry army-type loads. Braking was by hydraulic rear and mechanical front drums and equipment was to full service standards, so bearings and electrics were proofed against water and the wiring was suppressed.

A strange machine, but even odder was a

The Volugrafo Aermoto, in this instance with twin wheels, was also built with singles and intended for parachute drops. This one is back in Rome in 1944

tracked gun carrier built as an experiment. From the side the track looked like any other, but the complete assembly on each side could be moved up or down. Such was the total travel that the device stood normally on a 30-degree slope. It was driven by a 500 cc engine and could have been useful in the mountains, where it was often necessary to traverse lengthy slopes. If the driver pulled the lever the wrong way it no doubt fell over and rolled away.

Another unusual military machine was on the lines of the Trialce or the Mulo but with the rider enclosed, or semi-enclosed, with steel plating. The rear tyres were fitted with caterpillar tracks to aid traction and all wheels were discs. The machine was fitted with a gun and thus performed as a three-wheeled light tank.

Truly, Moto Guzzi were never short of an unusual solution to a problem.

Volugrafo Aermoto

Like the English, the Italians also built a motorcycle for throwing out of aeroplanes on the end of a parachute. Being Italian they made it a scooter.

The machine was really a miniature on the lines of the postwar Honda Monkey model, with small tyres on tiny pressed steel wheels. It was driven by a simple 125 cc single cylinder two-stroke engine, which had a flywheel magneto for ignition attached to the right end of the crankshaft.

The transmission was all chain and the gearbox contained two speeds and a double reduction gear, giving it dual ranges. The normal gearchange was by hand lever forward of the fuel tank and the range by one on the box. Speeds were 20 and 40 mph in high, dropping to 7 and 15 mph in low. A kickstarter was fitted on the right.

A duplex tubular rigid frame housed the mechanics, with everything well tucked in for stowage in the aircraft and for laying down on the ground. Suspension was minimal, having a bicycle-type front fork but with telescopic legs to give some small wheel movement. Comfort came either from a large pan saddle, pivoted at its nose and supported by a pair of tension springs or a hammock form seat.

The wheels were the most unusual feature of the machine as either singles or duals, front and rear, were used. The latter allowed the machine to stand upright alone and both types were discs with split rims. Both wheels had brakes, the rear operated by a pedal on the right. The handlebars rose up a long way because of the small dimensions of the rest of the machine. They were locked up by a pin and by releasing this could be folded back to suit the parachute container.

The Italian machine was not used in the numbers that the English ones were, but postwar the scooter idea led to Vespa and Lambretta, two makes that became synonymous around the world for the type.

9 Japan – were they all copies?

The Japanese motorcycle industry dates from Edwardian days, nearly died in the early 1920s and then recovered in the 1930s thanks to military expansion. In all that time the numbers built were minute, and even in the best year, 1940, production only just exceeded 3000 machines.

The industry was affected by the world-wide recession of the early thirties which was coupled with a balance of payments problem brought on by an excess of imports. Both civil and military riders sought to purchase foreign machines and the first were discouraged by tariffs that were raised as the thirties went by.

For the military the position was different as they had been using Harley-Davidson machines since World War I and wanted to continue doing so. The sales of the American machine were handled by Sankyo and due to a fall in the value of the dollar against the yen in 1929 an agreement came into being for Sankyo to build the machines working from Harley-Davidson drawings.

This was put into effect, at first using some parts from the USA, but by 1935 the machines were built entirely in Japan. Further commercial developments led to the machines being produced under the name Rikuo. In 1937 the tariff was increased by a factor of 7·5 and with the militarist

A Japanese ammunition carrier as captured on the Buna front in New Guinea. Adapted from motorcycle with disc wheels all round

government then in control this could not be evaded, even by the astute Harley-Davidson agents.

Thus the Rikuo became the machine for the Japanese Imperial army and in all some 18,000 were built. The machines were, of course, just like the Harley with a big 1200 cc side-valve, V-twin engine running slowly and pulling a high gear. The engine drove a three-speed gearbox and when used with a sidecar the driver had a reverse gear as well. A 750 cc version was also built as a solo.

Right **Same type of carrier ferrying men on a US air base in New Guinea past a B24 Liberator. Photo is marked not for use in Western Hemisphere or British Isles**

Below **The V-twin Harley-Davidson copy much used by Japanese forces and built in Japan as the Rikuo**

144

Engine lubrication was total loss, with an extra hand pump to supplement the mechanical one at speed or to replace it if it failed. Primary drive was by duplex chain and the clutch was foot controlled, as was the Harley. A rigid frame carried the engine and was fitted with Harley bottom-link front forks.

When the sidecar was attached (on the left) its wheel was driven by a shaft from the rear sprocket with rubber disc universal couplings at each end. A dog clutch enabled the drive to be disengaged. The sidecar body was well sprung on a leaf spring on each side and gave the passenger a better ride than the driver.

The outfit was able to cope with most conditions in the East, with a high mounted silencer on the right to help in streams. Given the correct handling it could outrun a Jeep on jungle tracks.

The Japanese had other home-built machines in small numbers, including three-wheelers similar to those built by the Italian firms. One such was the Toyo Kogyo; in essence a motorcycle back to the saddle with a two-wheeled chassis attached, as was usual with the type. On this various bodies or platforms could be built.

Other indigenous machines came from Asahi, Meguro and Cabton, all of whom built copies of European machines to a better or worse degree. Often the model copied was more from the vintage period but none was built in any great number. All were singles and all four-strokes.

Postwar it was different, with the first few signs of a rampant industry appearing in the early occupation years. Some incredibly crude machines were built, firms multiplied until they numbered a hundred or more, then came a cutthroat price war, until by 1960 a few firms ground out over one million machines in the 12 months. Then the Japanese began to export.

Japan – were they all copies?

10 Poland – the Sokol

The history of the Poles has been one of invasions, revolts and partitions. After the third in 1795 the country was controlled by others and it was only in 1919 that its boundaries were defined. These held for 20 short years until the country was invaded from east and west to once more be divided by others.

With this background it was hardly surprising that motorcycling was limited and it was not until the 1920s that there was much activity. Much of what little there was used imported engines and this supply came to a halt in 1939.

The first Polish machine was built around 1925 and, although really a Harley-Davidson copy, it had many problems. It was 1930 before the first batch of 100 was completed. They proved to be well out of date by then so no more were built.

It was decided to give the civilian market a miss and to produce a model for the army only. This was to be called the Sokol, eagle in Polish, and during the 1930s a total of 1000 were made, followed by a further 200 for the police and post office. All were to be built with sidecar attached.

The machines varied a little during production of the various batches they were made in. All used a number of components from England, including carburettors, pistons, chains and bearings, but for the rest the M111, as it was typed, was Polish built. For all that it still owed a great deal to USA design of the period.

The engine was a 995 cc V-twin with side valves on the right and light alloy cylinder heads.

Brest, France in 1940. The Polish Highland Rifle Brigade equipped with outfits possibly of Sokol manufacture although more likely Terrot or Gnome et Rhone

Machine-gun mounted on a Sokol M111 still resplendent with its eagle symbol on the tank

With a single carburettor feeding into the narrow angle of the vee the power was all low down and the engine pulled as only the type can. The gearbox was a three-speed unit with the gear lever on the right, while the multi-plate clutch was controlled by a foot pedal on the left in Harley style. In the same format the front brake lever and rear foot pedal were both on the right, while the throttle was a lever control on the left handlebar.

The frame was a massive duplex cradle with rigid rear and of tubular construction. The front forks (also tubular) were short leading links in Harley style with twin springs. Wheels were heavily constructed to cope with the loads and were interchangeable, the sidecar wheel being fitted with a brake. A spare was carried on the sidecar tail.

The sidecar chassis was attached at one point by a substantial leaf spring and the body was suspended on long semi-elliptics. It was long enough for the single passenger to sleep in, with storage space behind the seat squab.

When the Polish forces were defeated at least one outfit went into store and many years later turned up in Sweden. The others seem to have been destroyed or abandoned or may even have been captured by the Russians and finished their days in the east.

11 | Russia – some were home-made

A Russian TIZ-AM-600 fitted with skis to keep it mobile in the depths of the winter late in 1942

The Red Army used a large number of solo and sidecar machines during the war years and most of these were based on German designs. The political links between the two countries came just before the war began when a pact was signed and within days of war breaking out Russian forces advanced into Poland from the east as the German ones motored forward from the west.

With that country partitioned, Russia turned her attention to Finland and by early 1940 had forced a treaty from the Finns, who had to cede territory to the Reds. Later that year the Soviets mopped up the three small Baltic states and so built up a cushion between themselves and the German army. It failed to save them from Hitler's plans, because in 1941 he invaded Russia and drove forward nearly to Moscow before being rolled back, leaving thousands of vehicles for the Red Army to use.

Russian motorcycles were thin on the ground in the early days and to supplement them they were supplied with English models at first. Makes were Ariel, Matchless and Norton, and a few Velocettes, which must have been a puzzle to the Reds. Later came some 29,000 US machines, but these would have been easier to live with as a big V-twin was no stranger to Russian roads. Certain of their prewar models were based on Harley and Indian machines and were well suited to the vast distances and generally poor roads they had to contend with. In addition to the

149

Above **A column of Red Army despatch riders on the southern front in 1942. Machines are the L-300 model**

Right **M-72 sidecar outfits, ridden by Red Army scouts of the first motorcycle regiment of the guards, at work in the Russian battle zone**

imports there was a good number of captured German machines pressed into service, and with those the Russians were also more familiar.

Russian machines are named by a system that indicates their place of origin and their capacity in hundreds of ccs. The Promet factory in Leningrad thus produced the L-300, a 292 cc two-stroke single, which was built at the Kranii Oktobriya (Red October) works. Production ran from 1931 to 1940 and the machine was based on an old DKW with a pressed steel frame. It was used in considerable numbers by the Red Army.

M indicated Moskva and the ML-3 was the smallest of the DKW copies, being a 125 cc single-cylinder two-stroke coupled to a three-speed gearbox. The generator went on the right with the ignition points and the primary drive and foot pedals on the left. Final drive and rear brake were to the right, so the gearbox was a cross-over design as in the German original.

The frame was a cradle type with a rigid rear end and of tubular construction. The front forks were pressed steel blade girders with a single central suspension spring; wire spoke wheels

Russia – some were home-made

with small drum brakes were fitted. The remainder of the cycle parts copied the DKW items.

The ML-3 was only built for a year just before what was called the 'Great Patriotic War' broke out and was not supplied for military use; however, it is unlikely that it escaped some service.

A second DKW copy that appeared towards the end of the war was of the NZ350, which in Russia became the IZH-350. It again mirrored the German design, with single-cylinder two-stroke engine and, like it, had twin exhaust ports and systems copied down to the black-painted finish for the silencers. The engine was built in unit with a four-speed gearbox and this had both hand- and foot-change levers, the first attached to the right side of the fuel tank, the second on the left of the box.

The frame was built up from channel section steel pressings with rigid rear end and was fitted with blade girder front forks. The cycle parts were as on the German model, with a rear carrier and cantilever saddle and the resulting machine supplemented the L-300 models.

The M-72 flat twin was even nearer to its German counterpart for it was based on the BMW model R71. In 1939 it was made under licence at the Iskra Zavod in Moscow, but in 1941 the whole plant was moved to Irbitsk in the Urals. The M-72 was thus more modern than other models, for it had telescopic front forks, tubular cradle frame and plunger rear suspension. The power unit was the familiar flat twin, with side valves, twin carburettors and gear drive to the camshaft and dynamo both above the crankshaft.

The gearbox contained four speeds and a foot-change lever on the left plus an auxiliary lever for hand use on the right; the shaft drive to the rear wheel went on the same side, as did the sidecar when fitted. The cycle parts were all in the German style, with a saddle and rear carrier on early models and separate seats for driver and passenger plus a grab handle on later ones. The machine was used in both solo and sidecar forms.

A second 750 cc machine, typed the PMZ-A-750, was used in the same way and based on American V-twin techniques, with a side-valve engine driving a three-speed gearbox. The cycle side was as the early BMW, for the frame was built up from pressed steel sections, with forks of the trailing link type. The suspension medium was a quarter-elliptic leaf spring attached to the base of the steering column and connected by rods to the trailing links. It was well suited to the working terrain and used extensively by the Red Army along with the flat twins and two-stroke singles.

12 Sweden – neutral but not inactive

Engine and gearbox of the m42/SV, a copy of a 1935 Husqvarna, built by Monark, hence kneepad marking

Sweden remained neutral throughout World War 2 but was greatly affected by it, for in prewar days England and Germany had between them taken about half her total exports. On the outbreak of war the British established a blockade on the supply of iron ore to Germany and in reply some Swedish ships were sunk by U-boats.

As the months passed Sweden found herself between the Germans (occupying Norway) and the Russians (occupying Finland). Diplomacy of the highest order was needed to steer between the many problems that arose, and although a neutral, Sweden maintained armed forces.

At the start of the war the Swedes did as other countries and conscripted civilian machines. They also bought a number of DKW machines of 350 and 500 cc. Just as others had found, they discovered that this policy gave rise to two major problems. First, not all the machines would stand up to army use and soon fell by the wayside. Second, which arose following the first, the lack of spares and detailed knowledge made repair impossible when even maintenance gave them many problems.

To compound the Swedes' difficulties their home motorcycle industry had been run right down in the late 1930s so that Husqvarna, for instance, despite being one of the best-known Swedish firms, built no motorcycles at all for some years as all their capacity was taken up in producing rifles, pistols and armaments for the army.

153

The problem was given to the army vehicle office to solve, with orders to get a military machine into production. First thoughts centred on a German-style flat twin, but it was realized that to build such a type from scratch would take far too long by the time the development for production was complete.

Therefore it was decided that the simple single with an emphasis on easy servicing would be a much better answer. From that decision the need to get into production quickly led on to the idea of using a machine that had already been built and to just modify it where necessary to suit army use.

Left **The splayed out fork tubes of the m42/SV, a modification done to accommodate a revised front wheel**

Below **The m42/TV with overhead valves and interesting suspension designs at front and back**

Drive side of the m42/TV. Note spare plug in holder next to cylinder head

Finally two 500 cc Husqvarna models were chosen, these being the 112SV, with side valves, and the 112TV, with ohv, both models from 1935. The first was considered the simpler to put into production and so an initial batch of 300 was planned, Husqvarna agreeing to the use of their engineering drawings and tooling. The engine, gearbox and primary chaincase were made by Albin Motor in Kristinehamn, a marine engine manufacturer who up to then had not built air-cooled engines.

The frame and cycle parts were made by Monark in Varberg and they also assembled the complete machine. To avoid any hurt feelings the model was given the prosaic title of army motorcycle m/42.

The side-valve model was built with little change as the machines were needed quickly, and running a batch through the works was the fastest way of finding the manufacturing problems. The changes that were made concerned the wheels, which were made interchangeable, and the addition of leather panniers and a pillion seat. The most noticeable change was to the front forks, with the girder blade tubes splayed out beneath the lower crown to be much wider to accommodate the revised front wheel.

While this work was in hand the overhead-valve engine was modified in detail. This unit followed English lines and had the cylinder inclined forward a little in common with the side-valve motor, which was very similar. The crankcase was vertically split, with a built-up crankshaft that turned in a pair of roller bearings. The crank pin was pressed into the flywheels with expander plugs to lock it into place, while the big end

The NV-twin based on the m42/TV engine and built solely as a sidecar outfit with drive to both rear and chair wheels

began as an uncaged double row of rollers. These gave trouble, so later a cage was fitted and the pin modified.

The engine dimensions were 79 × 101 mm and the cylinder cast in iron with a pushrod tunnel integral with the casting. The head was in light alloy with bronze inserts for valve seats, sparking plug and fixing studs. These were four in number and anchored to sleeves in the crankcase to be free to screw up into the head. A system as used by BSA for their Gold Star engines.

The valve gear was straightforward, with the two cams on one shaft gear driven from the crankshaft. One of the changes made for army use was to delete the tappets and extend the pushrods to engage directly with the cam followers. At the same time adjusters were incorporated into the lower ends of the pushrods with access via a cover plate already incorporated in the cylinder casting to allow the valve clearances to be set.

At the top end the rockers pivoted on spindles in the head and each valve had dual springs and a hardened end cap. Access to them was via covers held by screws, which replaced the earlier screw-in caps. The actual valve timing was softer than usual to suit army use and this resulted in a lower power output but a more suitable running style.

Lubrication was dry sump, with the pump in the right crankcase. Ignition was by magneto driven by chain from the camshaft. The dynamo was mounted on top of it and at first Bosch equipment was used. Once the 1200 sets to hand were used up there were no more available so from then on they were made by SEM to fit in place of the German items. The same problem arose with the side-mounted Amal carburettor as only 1200 of them could be had; from then on they had to be made from the solid. This was not very satisfactory so one of the first orders received by Amal after the war was for a batch for Sweden. At the same postwar time the opportunity was taken to fit air filters as previously these had seldom been used.

A further refinement was added to cope with the poor quality fuel, which was often all that was available and which made starting very difficult in the cold. A small tank of good petrol was carried on the rear frame and this had a built-in pump. It connected to the inlet tract, so the drill was one stroke on the pump and a swing on the kickstarter, which usually brought results.

The engine drove a three-speed gearbox by chain, contained in a cast light alloy case, on the left. The case joint was on the horizontal centreline of the two sprockets and so much less prone to oil leakage than many of its contemporaries. The gearbox was in the English style, with the final drive chain also on the left, and was operated by a rather crude heel-and-toe foot pedal. This connected to an external positive stop mechanism under a pressed steel cover and in turn this moved the gears. In addition it was linked to the clutch worm so that this was automatically raised when the gear pedal was used.

The rigid frame for the side-valve model was built up from two sections, the front one of welded construction, and was fitted with conventional girders with central spring. For the ohv model this was completely changed after the first three prototypes had been built and tested. The new frame was built in two sections with the front an open diamond with the engine tying the

Above **The offset six-speed and reverse gearbox of the NV, bevel driven from the crankshaft and lined up to the rear wheel**

Right **Suecia Armé model built in small numbers for the Swedish army**

down and seat tubes together. To this was bolted the rear part, with each side in a Z form with the upper tube running back to support the rear mudguard tail, pillion seat and panniers.

From the centre of the upper tube a plunger assembly was vertically mounted. Its lower end connected to the junction of the lower and diagonal tubes. Each plunger comprised a rod, slider and compression and rebound springs and the assemblies were bolted to the frame so they could be moved fore and aft. This enabled the chain tension to be set and allowed the wheel spindle to be fixed to the sliders in a very rigid manner.

The front forks were also new and set wide, as on the side-valve model, to accommodate the hubs. The girder blades were tubular in construction and the top links were extended forward to actuate the suspension springs. There were two of these each in a housing attached to the girder blade, with a rod rising from the assembly to attach to the lengthened top link. In each spring assembly went a spring adjuster and hydraulic damping with a needle valve to vary the effect.

Each wheel comprised a hub spoked into a rim with the brake drum connected by six pegs working in rubber inserts in the hub. The brakes were single leading shoe drums and the rear was operated by a pedal whose shaft ran through the chaincase.

For the side-valve model a normal pattern headlamp was fitted and protected by a crash bar, while the speedometer, which was driven from the front wheel, was mounted on top of the forks. For the ohv model the headlamp was set back between the wider fork blades and had the speedometer head mounted in the rear of its shell. The crash bar was deleted, but a convoy lamp was added on top or to one side of the headlamp. The model was finished off with saddle, pillion seat and leather panniers.

For use in the winter the machines were fitted with skis plus a hand lever for gear changing, enabling the rider to keep both feet on the boards all the time. This fitting and the techniques of using it was used by all the Scandinavian countries at one time or another.

Some 3000 model m/42TV machines were built during the later part of the war and the m/42 stayed in service use until 1965. Once its development bugs had been sorted out it proved to be a reliable workhorse and ideal for the job it had to do.

In addition to this basic model the Swedes were also attracted to the idea of a sophisticated BMW-style sidecar outfit and a project to build one began in 1942. The job went to Nymans Verkstader, or NV, in Uppsala and the design of engine and gearbox was by Folke Mannerstedt on a consultant basis.

The first stage was to build a prototype or two, and with the m/42 already in production it made good sense to use some of its engine parts. The result became a narrow-angle V-twin using the 500 cc top half giving it a capacity of one litre. The cylinder heads were modified so that a single carburettor could feed into a manifold in the vee, and the exhaust ran on the right.

The engine itself was really very conventional, with the magneto tucked in behind it and a chain drive from the timing gear on the right. Construction was traditional and from it came 36 bhp at 4000 rpm.

From then on it became unconventional. As the specification called for shaft drive and sidecar use only the designers chose to turn the drive at the crankshaft. This was duly done in a housing on the left of the crankcase and from this the gearbox extended to the rear. Its shafts lay along the machine and carried a total of six forward speeds and a reverse. Control was by a pair of levers mounted on the left side of the petrol tank.

The drive shaft emerged from the rear of the gearbox nicely offset to line up with the rear bevel box. The fact that the gears were well away from the machine centre-line mattered not at all with a sidecar, so the layout was totally logical.

The bevel box turned the drive once more and drove the rear wheel and a cross-shaft to the sidecar wheel, which was ahead of the rear thanks to the gearing.

The frame was a cradle with tubular and pressed steel members and the front forks were telescopic. Both wheels had massive drum brakes joined to steel rims by very short spokes. The brakes were hydraulic in operation and the wheels shrouded by wide valanced mudguards. Separate seats were provided for driver and passenger and the headlamp was tucked in between the fork legs for protection. The speedometer, on the other hand, was clipped to the top of the forks and driven from the front wheel.

Few of these machines were built and on trial they displayed all the virtues and vices of the type – very good in the right hands and lethal for anyone else. When the Jeep became available the army forgot its special sidecar and went for four wheels.

Of the other Swedish companies, Rex did not supply any machines to the army during the war but Suecia did. These were of prewar design with a MAG side-valve engine of 82 × 94 mm dimensions and 496 cc capacity. The construction was rather old-fashioned in an English style, but was well built with a Burman four-speed gearbox and Bosch electrics.

The cycle parts were conventional, with girder forks, rigid frame and drum brakes. The finish was appropriate for the services and the model was known as the *Arme* type. It came as a solo or could be fitted with a sidecar chassis on the left; however, this was not totally rigidly connected as it lacked a fixing to the steering head region. The body went on to a pair of semi-elliptic springs and the wheel on a stub axle.

Although well made, these models were relatively few in number and the m/42 remained the machine for the Swedish army during the conflict and after.

13 | Switzerland – an active industry

The Swiss retained their traditional neutrality during the war but still had an army that was fully mobilized as soon as war was declared. Within two weeks all able-bodied adults of both sexes were enrolled in ARP or defence work and measures taken to round up suspects. The authorities were not having their country a base for espionage and all this activity created a need for motorcycles along with everything else.

The machines used came from the major Swiss firms of Condor, Motosacoche and Universal and were cast in the traditional mould of the 1930s. Motosacoche supplied engines to many other firms, including Condor, as well as building complete machines, but Universal made their own side-valve V-twins of 680 and 990 cc.

Late in the war Condor produced a flat twin that was very much in the style of a BMW or Zundapp. It had a 580 cc engine with side valves and drove a dual-range, four-speed gearbox with shaft drive to the rear wheel. The engine was smooth, with electrics and carburettor under covers, and it was installed in a girder forks rigid frame.

In addition to the flat twins the army no doubt used some of the smaller singles from Allegro and Zehnder. The later (associated with the German Standard make from the early 1930s) were mainly two-stroke powered. Postwar plans were cancelled when the designer died suddenly.

14 | USA – 'the motorcycle that won the war'

The American motorcycle firms became involved in the war long before Pearl Harbor and well prior to the Lease-Lend bill of March 1941. Within a few months of the outbreak they had received orders for substantial numbers from both the English and French armies, who found themselves short of most items needed in modern warfare.

The bulk of the machines supplied to Europe and later used by American and Canadian forces came from the two main firms and were in one very set pattern. To European eyes the large and heavy V-twins with their foot clutch and hand gearchange were a strange sight, but they were very well developed and suited to their tasks.

The ability to stand up to mile after mile of steady cruising, often in a high ambient temperature, was what kept the two firms in business and the same qualities were just the job for a service machine. For this use the performance would be lowered a little to ensure that the machine continued to run in the worst of environments even when neglected and abused. All the pretty bits were left off, anything that stuck out was either protected or made strong enough not to bend and the resulting machine called up. On enlistment it went through the quarter-master's stores, as did all recruits, and drew its army gear. For the motorcycle this was normally more weight in the form of gun holster, ammunition box and carrier bags.

At the other end of the scale there were a

Military Motorcycles of World War 2

An American in Europe. Decorated officer inspects 74-inch UA Harley-Davidson to British specification on English soil; note the 16 in. wheels. Soon to get much dirtier. Strong, they were

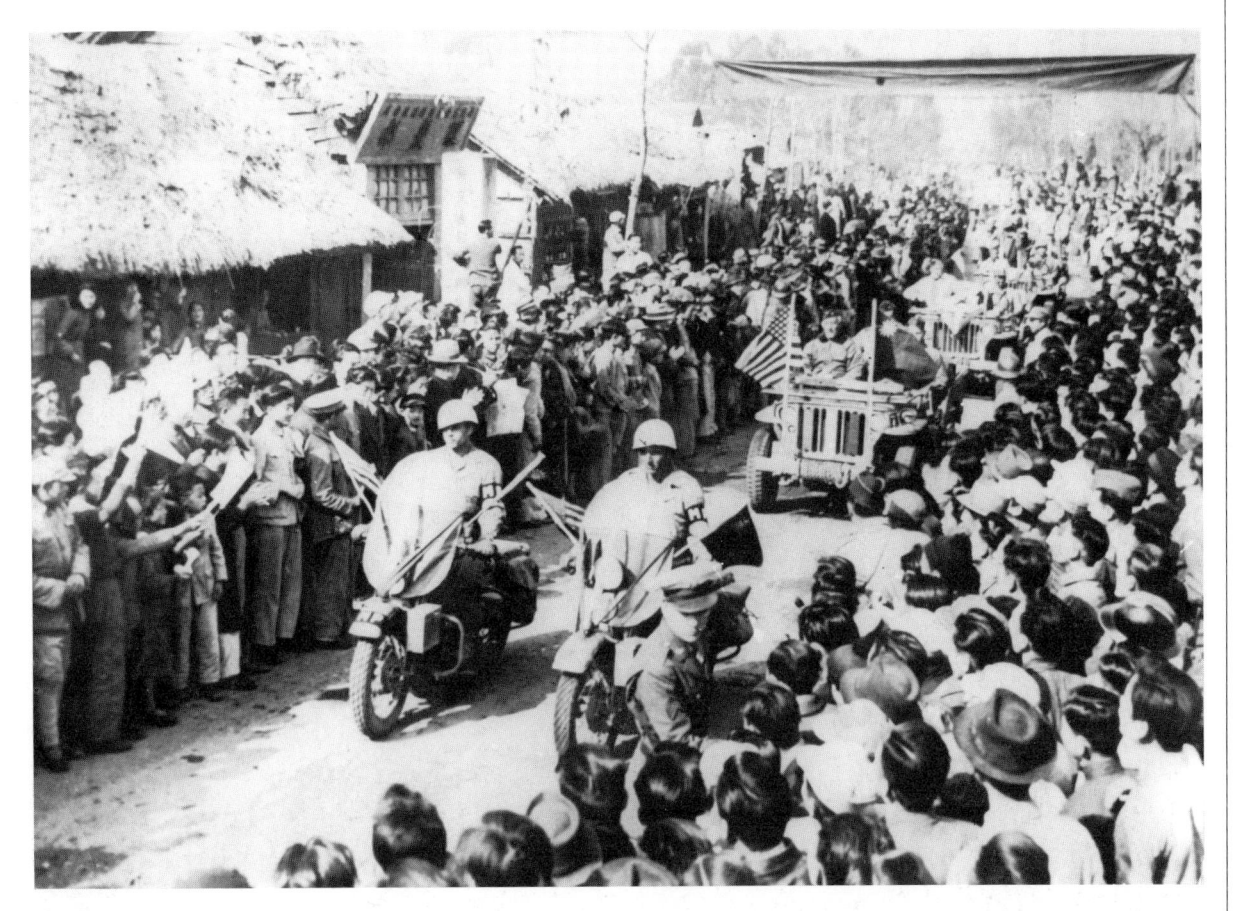

couple of lightweights. One was essentially a means of running about the base more quickly and a useful adjunct on airfields, where distances, even across a hangar, tend to be large.

Chinese civilians in Kunming greeting the first convoy to use the Ledo and Burma roads from India with two WLA Harley-Davidsons in the van; date 23rd January 1945

USA – 'the motorcycle that won the war'

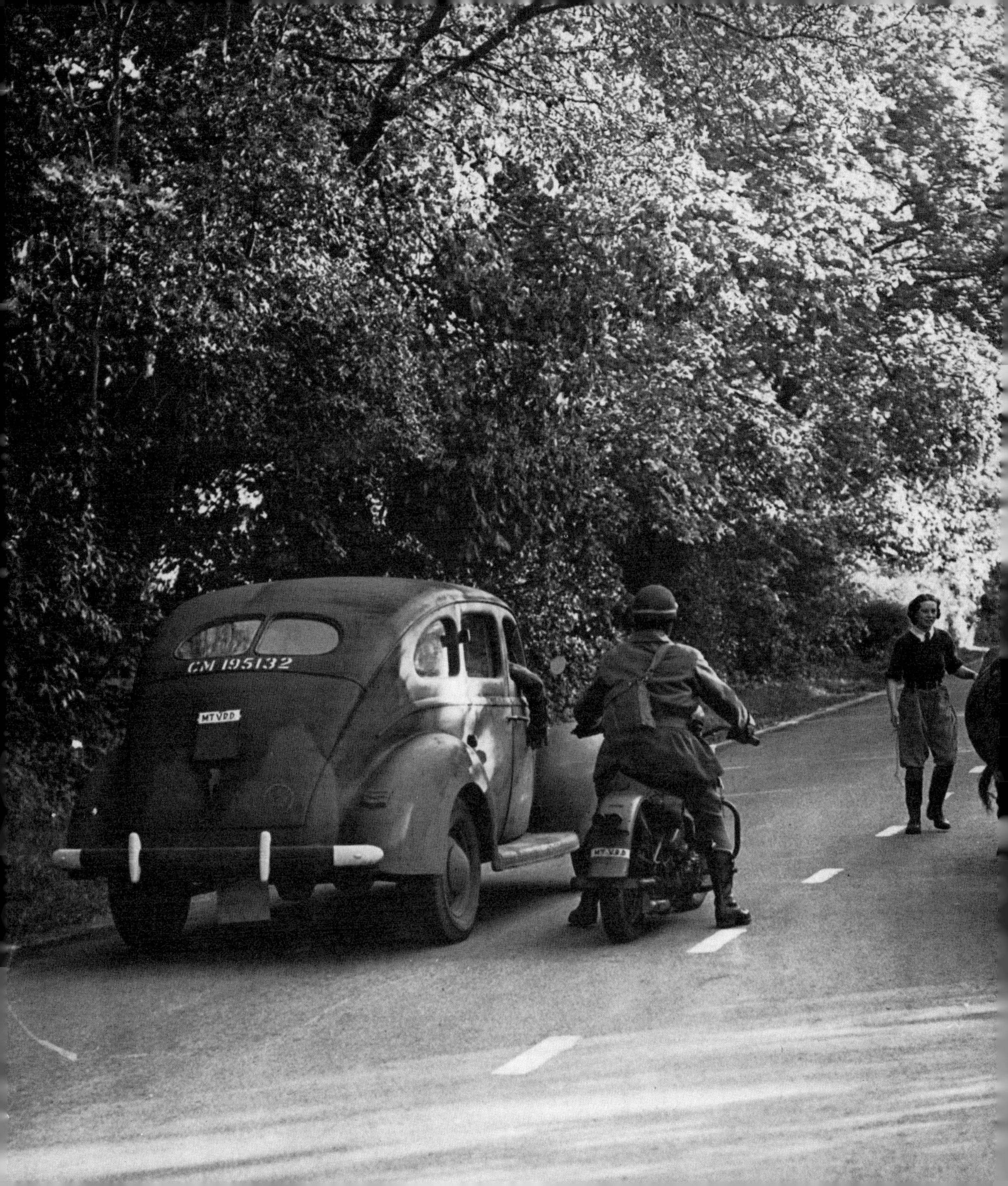
GM 195132

Sussex in 1942 with the Women's Land Army driving their cows while a convoy passes. The motorcycle is a WLC Harley-Davidson to British specification

The second was more of a scooter and designed to be dropped by parachute to support airborne troops in the same manner as some of the English babies.

After the war many of the V-twins stayed in Europe and did sterling service in those austere days. Exciting they were not, but with few new machines to be had anything with two wheels and an engine was worth having. In time they were discarded, but not before a good few civilians had come to cherish the rugged and dependable American V-twin.

Crosley

In Cincinnati, Ohio, in 1939 there lived one Powel Crosley, who was a busy fellow. He owned the local radio station, where he did his stint as disc jockey, he was involved with the local football team, the Cincinnati Reds, and he began to build minicars using a Wankesha twin-cylinder engine.

Came Pearl Harbor and he decided to enter motorcycle production as well and so came to build a few prototypes for the army to evaluate. The result was rather unusual.

The machine had a flat twin engine with side valves no doubt taken from the car. The gearbox was thus built in unit with the engine and its gear lever was of the car type. It was cranked to emerge beneath the pan saddle on the right, so a gear shift looked like the rider was having a scratch.

The frame was tubular and fitted with telescopic front forks while the wheels came from the car. Both were disc and the rear one was overhung and came complete with hub plate to cover the fixing nuts. Oddest feature was the petrol tank, which was formed as the rear mudguard. A diaphragm pump driven from the camshaft and positioned at the top front of the

USA – 'the motorcycle that won the war'

165

The Crosley built in Cincinnati for the US army to evaluate but not taken up

engine lifted the petrol to the carburettor.

The capacity was given as 580 cc, the engine was of the wet sump lubrication type and a large car-style battery went under the seat. Due to its car origins it had shaft drive to the rear wheel, but the US army decided to stick with the Harleys and Indians it knew and understood.

Cushman

These machines were built in Lincoln, Nebraska, and the best-known model was a scooter intended for airborne use by paratroops. It was a very basic model and so disposable when the situation warranted it, but for rapid dispersal once the men reached the ground a light motorcycle was most suitable.

After his drop the soldier could mount up and be with his group in moments. They could then move as a body or separate and in minutes be well away from the landing zone, either attacking their target or hidden under cover ready for action. As the machines were small and light it was easy enough for the men to handle them over obstacles if necessary, and this aspect was helped if they worked in pairs.

The Cushman used a 244 cc single-cylinder four-stroke engine of an industrial type so had side valves, fan cooling and a flywheel magneto. In scooter fashion the engine went beneath the rider's saddle and behind it was mounted a two-speed gearbox. This was chain driven, with the centrifugal clutch on the right; an unguarded final drive chain went on the left to the rear wheel.

A cylindrical fuel tank was set across the machine above the gearbox so all the machinery was kept in one place. The frame was simple, with a channel member running along one side, round the rear wheel and back along the other. A steering head was formed at the front and from it panels ran down and back in scooter format to provide an apron, footboards and small leg-shields.

Two loops ran up and over from one side of the main frame to the other. One went ahead of the engine and supported the saddle nose while the other went at the rear, just ahead of the rear wheel spindle. The two loops were joined by horizontal bars that served to protect the engine and to provide a mounting for the saddle springs.

The front forks were unsprung and had welded on handlebars and a reinforcing strut for each leg. The wheels were tiny with split hubs and fat 6·00 × 6 in. balloon tyres in scooter style. The rear carried a small drum brake and both had simple flat mudguards. Behind the rear wheel the frame had a pintle hook for towing and the rear loop had machine parachute attachment rings. Crude and simple it may have been but it served a purpose.

From the same stable came two other models, both with the same form of engine and transmission. One was a sidecar, but the other was more unusual and, although it had three wheels; two were at the front, a single one at the rear giving the tractive drive. Useful for carrying a fair quantity of goods, and much of the military machine is just that – the movement of men and materials.

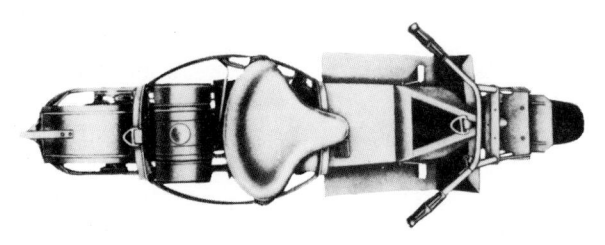

Plan view of the Cushman airborne scooter for use by paratroops

Harley-Davidson

Harley-Davidson is as American as blueberry pie or the Fourth of July and the bulk of the machines from Milwaukee built for the army were in their traditional V-twin style. Only for a brief moment did they deflect from their normal path to produce a flat twin BMW copy.

The first wartime order came not from Washington but from England, for some 5000 machines with a note for delivery 'as quick as you can, a bomb or two has just been dropped on Coventry'. Appreciating the British flair for understating their case H-D quickly came up with the WLA model based on the 45 cu. in. machine that dated from 1929.

Old it might have been but it was tough to the degree that only Harley owners took for granted and needed few changes to make it suitable for army service and the mud of Europe. It had been introduced as a medium-weight model of 750 cc to run alongside the big 1200 cc V-twin; large capacities being typical of American practice. Also typical was the use of side valves and modest compression ratios, so the capacity was needed to give them an acceptable performance. What it also brought was reliability, tremendous low-down torque and low-wear rates, all very good features for a service motorcycle.

The engine of the WLA was in the classic narrow-angle, V-twin mould. Bore and stroke came in inch measurements of $2\frac{3}{4} \times 3\frac{13}{16}$ to give the 45 cu. in. capacity that is the American equivalent of the 750 cc European figure. The compression ratio was a modest 5:1 and the power around 25 bhp at 4500 rpm with peak torque at 3000 rpm.

Engine construction was on the heavy side. The iron cylinders and light alloy heads were well finned to ensure adequate cooling even during lengthy low-speed running in bottom gear. The valves went on the right with the two exhaust pipes joining low down to run back to the single

USA – 'the motorcycle that won the war'

Military Motorcycles of World War 2

silencer. The carburettor was a single Linkert that fed a manifold between the barrels.

Ignition was by coil, with both plugs firing simultaneously and the generator set above the crankcase in front of the forward cylinder. The ignition setting was not controlled by a lever as on English machines but by a twistgrip and this went on the right handlebar. At least on some early machines the throttle went on the left along with the front brake lever; the idea of this was that the rider could loose off his sidearm, or even a sub-machine gun, while controlling his steed with his left hand.

The idea proved to be less than practical when tried and to represent a grave hazard to the rider and any of his comrades in the vicinity. After a year or so the controls were switched over to fall into line with convention everywhere.

Lubrication was dry sump with the oil carried above the engine in one half of what appeared to be the petrol tank. Actually it was two tanks bolted together with petrol in the left and oil in the right. The oil pumps both had bleeds to drip oil on to the primary and final drive chains. This was a little messy but kept the chains happy. The primary chaincase was thus not oiltight and simply a cover for the chain, sprockets and clutch.

The bottom half of the engine was strongly built, with the heavy flywheels carried in a vertically split light alloy crankcase. The primary drive went on the left with a duplex chain driving the clutch and three-speed gearbox. The clutch was controlled by a foot pedal on the left with an over-centre spring so that it could be put into the disengaged position and left if the rider needed to use his foot to support the machine. A hand-operated clutch lever was fitted later and went on the right bar to suit the original control configuration.

The gear change was by hand with the lever on the left in a gate bolted to the side of the petrol tank. The gearbox had cross-over drive with the final chain on the right. It ran inboard

Left **Harley-Davidson model WL late in 1939 on field manoeuvres in Texas. The machine is a militarized civilian model**

Below left **Harleys on patrol during training in Southern Rhodesia in 1941. 1939 750 cc model**

Below **A Harley-Davidson WLA posed for the camera in 1942 – or, the rider will be in trouble as his gun lacks a magazine**

USA – 'the motorcycle that won the war'

of the substantial kickstart lever with its usual Harley folding bicycle pedal for the rider to tread on. A hefty clutch release arm went just ahead of it.

The frame was rigid with a heavy steel pressing bolted to it to protect the crankcase and gearbox. This steel plate was of channel form for stiffness and was extended on the right to protect both the silencer and the rear chain. The front forks were Harley bottom link with twin springs and numerous grease nipples.

The wheels were shod with 4·00 × 18 in. tyres normally, but a wider section was fitted when the machine was used in the desert. Brakes were 6 in. diameter drums with single leading shoes, the front operated by hand and the rear by a pedal on the right. This sat way above the footboards provided for the rider's feet so judicious use was none too easy, especially if the clutch was being operated at the same time.

The WLA had its speedometer and lights switch in the normal Harley position in a console on top of the tanks. The speedometer went to 120 mph but a plate warned the rider not to exceed 65 mph. The ignition and lighting switch

Rolling down the ramp on a WLA, most likely in training as soldiers in combat are less clean

was flanked by warning lights for oil pressure and generator.

In most respects the machine was as the civilian model with extra equipment fitted. However, the compression ratio was lower than standard and a very large and restrictive air filter was attached to the carburettor by hose from its housing on the left below the saddle. To this already heavy machine were added wide clearance mudguards, to avoid problems in mud, and the military gear.

This added up as for a start there was a holster attached to the right side of the front forks to carry either a rifle or sub-machine gun, and it was matched on the left by a small ammunition box. A screen was provided for the rider with a small transparent section above a large apron. In front of it went a headlamp with a masked lamp above that and a pilot lamp attached to the top of the front mudguard. Legshields could be fitted and both front and rear crash-bars were usual. Between them they allowed the machine to be dropped on its side without worry as to damage. At the rear was a carrier on top of the rear mudguard and pannier bags on each side.

In all it weighed some 540 lb dry and ran in typical American fashion, happy up to around 60 mph day-in, day-out and best run on long straight roads. Not so good on bumpy corners, it could however slog round nearly all in top gear and pull back to its amble along the boulevard. The handling may not have been to the standards of the English models but the Harley pan saddle gave the rider an easy time so over anything like a long distance the Harley would be the less tiring – as one would expect, for the make was designed for such use. Off-road the minute 4 in. ground clearance was a problem.

The major part of H-D's wartime production comprised the WLA, but in addition some 20,000 very similar WLC machines were built for the Canadian forces. While similar they were not the same, but then there were usually some detail changes from one contract to the next for the

Harley-Davidson WLA with most of the standard military fittings

basic WLA. Many WLA machines went to Russia and the result of their experiences was the WSR prototype built with sidecar with single seat, screen and spare wheel carried on the back of the body. (The firm also built sidecars and supplied some of these hitched to their 74 in. V-twin

Unusual 74 cu. in. model with rigged gun bracket, qd front wheel and buddy seat. 1940 photo

USA – 'the motorcycle that won the war'

Left **A 1940 Harley-Davidson WLC in full flight under British army control**

Below **The Harley-Davidson XA flat twin modelled on the BMW R12 and pictured in 1943**

for special services. The machines were little altered from the civilian specification, but had lowered gearing and compression ratios to aid their job and increase reliability. There were also a few 61 in. ohv models for the navy.)

There were other prototypes for various jobs, but only one ever reached the point of initial production. This was the XA, which was simply a copy of the German BMW R12 used by them in the Western Desert. Impressed by the success of these machines the army buyers issued a specification for a similar model and Harley took the easy route by measuring a captured R12.

The engine was thus a horizontal flat twin with side valves and twin carburettors. Bore and stroke were equal at $3\frac{1}{16}$ in. so the capacity was 45 cu. in. and the compression ratio 5·7:1. An air cleaner went on top of the gearbox housing, which was bolted directly to the rear of the crankcase, and the transmission featured the footchange and transverse kickstart pedal both on the left, as on the German model. The gearbox had four speeds.

Naturally shaft drive was used and this went on the right, as did the normal BMW hand lever for gear selection which supplemented the footchange. The frame was a tubular cradle with plunger rear suspension, but at the front Harley stuck to their standard leading link forks. They did, however, add hydraulic damping in the form of a unit attached to the right fork leg. They also kept their usual footboards, but added footrests aft of them plus heat shields behind the cylinders to keep boots away and to protect the fins.

Most of the other details were as on the WLA, but the panniers were shallower to clear the plunger boxes and both sides of the petrol tank carried fuel as lubrication was wet sump. Equipment included the front fork gun holster and matching ammunition box, while a desert version was fitted with disc wheels.

In all 1000 were built for the US army to evaluate and five more for the Canadians. The XA showed again the pitfalls of copying, for Harley

Riding the XA in 1983 in England is owner and restorer Jim Dowdall who fetched some spares from California

did not have the years of experience with the flat twin engine that BMW had. The lack of a sludge trap in the crankshaft, which meant frequent oil changes, or big ends was one quirk.

The XA was meant for solo use but a few were fitted with a chair and known as the XS model. The early problems were nothing that could not have been sorted by the factory, but by the time the evaluation was near complete the war had moved on. In the end it was decided that the Jeep was the vehicle to go for so the XA was dropped ... and Harley-Davidson continued to grind out their stock V-twin.

Indian

In America only two makes stayed in production from Edwardian to postwar times, one being the Indian. Its fortunes waxed and waned several times during this period and in 1939 it was none too well placed to fulfil many military orders.

The reason behind this lay in the years of the Depression, which had seen equipment sold off to pay bills and no replacements bought. The tooling left was thus insufficient and much of it too antiquated for high-volume production. New machine tools became increasingly hard to obtain as the war spread and in total this situation greatly affected the machines that Indian produced.

Their first involvement with the war in Europe was a French order for 5000 of the Chief model 340B fitted with a sidecar. This used the massive 74 cu. in. V-twin engine with side valves in the new 1940 frame with plunger rear suspension. The front forks remained much as they had been since the very early days of the company, with a short trailing link connected by a stay to a leaf spring mounted to the underside of the steering column. The spring ran forward from this point to act as a quarter elliptic.

The engine and transmission were very similar to the Harley-Davidson (as they had been for many a year). Common to both makes was the single carburettor attached to the manifold feeding into the vee of the cylinders, foot clutch, three-speed gearbox, final drive chain on the right and footboards. Detail differences lay in the gearchange lever on the right for the Indian, the method of holding the clutch out and minor details.

Line of Indian 741B models being finished at the Springfield, Massachusetts, factory before dispatch to Britain

The tanks were split, with the right one also carrying the oil, and a tank panel held the speedometer and lights switch. As on the Harley, ignition was by coil with the distributor mounted on top of the timing chest and able to turn to advance the timing. In the same way the kickstart carried a folding bicycle pedal at its working end and the rear brake was controlled by a pedal mounted above the right footboard.

To go with this hefty machine there was a single seat sidecar mounted on a tubular chassis, but the first batch to be delivered, nearly half the order, failed to reach Europe. The machines were freighted by ship and it is believed that this was sunk by torpedo action.

Early in the war, and well before Pearl Harbor, the US authorities asked the factory to submit prototypes for military testing. With the precarious position of their tooling Indian had no option but to utilize parts from their production range for this exercise, but the result worked well.

The machine was at first known as the 640, then the 640A and finally as the 741A. It was, by American standards, a small-engined model built very much in the style of the USA motorcycle of that period and tough and reliable. To this end the compression ratio was low, the valve timing mild and the breathing restricted, so not many horses came from the 640's 45·44 cu. in. motor. The 741, although similar, used a 30·06 cu. in. engine version. Those that did drove the three-speed gearbox via a primary chain on the left with the final one on the right.

The gearchange was by right hand, the clutch by left foot, the throttle by left hand and the ignition advance by right hand. Nearly all the points of the 74 in. model were the same on the 30, except that the frame was rigid and the forks girders with a central barrel spring to take the load and friction dampers to control it. In addition the forks were extended by $1\frac{1}{2}$ in. to give the machine a little more, much needed, ground clearance.

To this standard American cycle were added some extras for the military. A rifle holster went on the right side of the front forks with an ammunition box on the left, while at the rear went leather saddlebags.

A massive air cleaner went on the left beneath the pan saddle and the speedometer was mounted on top of the front forks, where it was driven by the front wheel. An ammeter and switch went on a small panel mounted on the front of the two tanks ahead of the filler caps and a headlight and convoy light were fitted. A hefty front crash bar allowed the machine to be dropped to ground in a hurry without bending anything of note, while for more leisurely moments there was a rear stand.

The performance of the 640 or 741A was nothing special – in fact it carried a plate to tell the rider not to exceed 60 mph – but it was rugged and it kept going.

It was soon joined by a larger version first known as the 640B and later as the 741B. This used a low compression ratio Sports Scout engine of 45 cu. in. and was much preferred by the US forces. The extra power gave it a perfor-

1200 Indian Chief in Scotland in 1942 with Polish forces. The sidecar nose has a map of Poland painted on its top

USA – 'the motorcycle that won the war'

175

An Indian Chief and sidecar in 1941 and prepared to repel boarders

mance suited to American traffic conditions and their riders were more used to the larger capacity model.

In Europe 500 cc was thought large enough, so it was the 741A that England ordered from Indian late in 1941. 5000 machines plus a few Chiefs with sidecars were called for and kept the Indian works hard at it. After the war they were to prove to be a ready source for English enthusiasts and were not subject to the then normal high tariffs that applied to new machines. The snag at first was that while machines were sold off spares were not, so that even a sparking plug or a gasket set was a problem. In time the army let go of its stocks and the V-twins ran on for a good few years.

When the War Department asked Harley and Indian for a new prototype military model Harley copied the BMW flat twin, but Indian came up with something rather different. This was their model 841. It had a transverse 45 cu. in. V-twin engine with the cylinders set at 90 degrees, and was a style to be used postwar by the Japanese Lilac and the Italian Guzzi.

The engine was designed in the usual military form with restricted power output and an emphasis on durability. So the alloy heads on the iron barrels gave a low compression ratio and the two carburettors only allowed a modest flow of mixture in for combustion. Both were connected by hose to a single air cleaner mounted above the gearbox.

The valves were at the front of the engine, so the inlet manifolds ran forward to them. Under the timing cover lay a train of gears which drove each camshaft, the double oil pump for the dry sump system, a timed engine breather and, via a couple of idler gears, the generator. This last lay in the vee of the cylinders and drove the coil ignition distributor from its rear end.

The gearbox bolted to the back of the engine and contained four speeds selected by a rocking foot pedal on the left. Clutch control was by hand with the lever mounted on the right, while the throttle went on the left along with the front brake lever. The rear brake pedal went on the right and footboards were provided for the rider's feet.

The rear wheel was driven by an exposed shaft and both wheels carried 8 in. drum brakes. The front rode in girders with a telescopic appearance as the blades were formed from oval section tubing. Suspension was by twin springs with a hydraulic damper mounted between them. At the rear went plunger units, the frame being of tubular construction with a single top tube and the others duplex.

The fuel tank had twin fillers and a small tank-top panel, while the oil tank went under the saddle. The front forks carried a headlamp with a convoy light on top of it and a front wheel-driven speedometer. A mirror was clipped to the left handlebar. Equipment included a pan saddle, a rear carrier, pannier bags and double rear lamps.

Some 1056 examples of this model were built and plans laid for full production, until the War Department switched to Jeeps as its main service vehicle. The same fate befell a design exercise to produce a lightweight model for paratroops.

At the end of the war Indian found that they

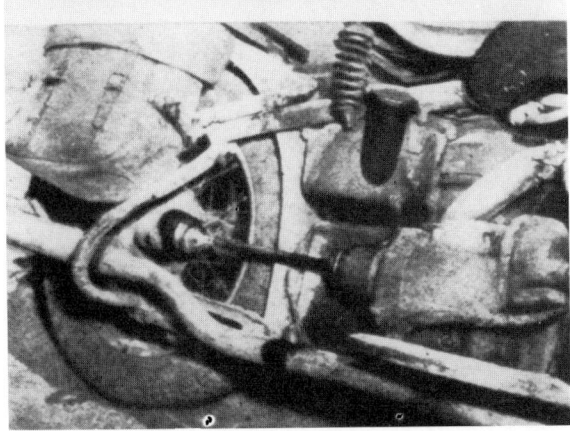

Above **The Indian model 841 with transverse V-twin engine and shaft drive**

Left **The 841 pictured during its army tests, the top photo shows the vee layout clearly**

had supplied just over 42,000 machines to the services, not counting the French order but including some 9000 that found their way to Russia. The machines continued to run on in civilian hands for a good few years as the need of the late 1940s was for reliable transport, just what the tough V-twin was.

Simplex

This company in New Orleans, Louisiana, was in business for a good number of years producing the most basic of transport for people who wanted to be powered over short distances. During and after the war they built the Servi-Cycle, which changed but little over some 20 years.

The machine was unusual in both engine and transmission. The power unit was a 7·5 cu. in. or 125 cc two-stroke that owed more to industrial practice than motorcycling. The cylinder was cast in light alloy in one with the head and this carried twin sparking plugs fired by a special flywheel magneto on the right. A sleeve provided a running surface for the deflector-type piston and the connecting rod was in light alloy with a twin ball-bearing big end.

The crankshaft was overhung and ran in three ball-bearing mains. It was also ported to act as

USA – 'the motorcycle that won the war'

the inlet. The carburettor, which fed it, was sited behind and on the same level as the crankshaft. The carburettor was a car type with butterfly throttle and was fitted with a choke. The exhaust system began as a flange bolted to the barrel and from this a pipe went down and to the rear on the left.

If the engine was unusual the transmission was more so, for both primary and final drives were by belt, and the drive ratios could be varied under pedal control. The device that did this was mounted up under the saddle and driven from the right side of the engine, the belt sitting between crankcase and magneto. From it a second belt went to a large pulley attached to the left side of the rear wheel.

At the junction the input and output pulleys had inner flanges that could be moved under pedal control to contract and expand the effective pulley diameter, thus altering the gearing. The pedal could also be used to hold the drive pulley clear of its belt to act as a clutch.

There was no kickstarter so a push was needed to get going, but this was no penalty to the services, although in later years a crude quadrant and gear were added. In addition the drive was made more automatic with a centrifugal drum clutch and ratio change being adopted.

The frame was simple with duplex loops running back to join at the rigid rear end. Front forks were American-style bottom link with very limited movement, so most comfort came from the big pan saddle. The wheels were large with 26 × 2·5 in. tyres and only the rear was braked with a small drum controlled by a pedal on the right.

Direct lighting was provided and fuel was carried in twin tanks each with a filler cap. A filter was fitted to the fuel tap but no reserve and the rider was instructed that half a gallon would be trapped in the left side, so if you ran out you laid the machine on its right for five seconds.

Being an American machine it came with footboards and a front crash bar and postwar ones at least had a prop stand. No doubt in wartime it was just left laid on the bar until needed once again. A good indication of the efficiency of the belt system was a postwar three-wheeled version built as a 4 cwt. delivery truck. Both types were much used by businesses with large grounds in and around New Orleans and they and the army found them A1 at their job.

Epilogue

A 1946 picture of machines from the NFS and other Civil Defence organizations on sale at a Surrey dump. Many thousands of service models were sold the same way

Specifications

Country	Austria			
Make	**Puch**	**Puch**	**Puch**	**Puch**
Model	**200**	**250 S4**	**350 GS**	**125 T**
No. cylinders	1 split	1 split	1 split	1 split
Bore (mm)	2 × 45	2 × 45	48 & 55[1]	2 × 38
Stroke (mm)	62·8	78	83·4	55
Capacity (cc)	199·8	248	349[2]	124·7
Compression ratio (to 1)	5·0	6·5	6·2	6·5
Power: bhp	5·8	10·5	13·5	5·2
@ rpm	4000	4300	4000	4500
Valve type	piston	piston	piston	piston
No. gears	3	4	4	3
Top gear ratio		4·52[3]	4·32	7·07
Front tyre (in.)	3·00 × 19	3·00 × 19[4]	3·50 × 19	3·00 × 19
Rear tyre (in.)	3·00 × 19	3·00 × 19[4]	3·50 × 19	3·00 × 19
Front suspension	girder	girder	girder	girder
Rear suspension	rigid	rigid	link	rigid
Petrol tank (litre)	8·5	12·5	12·5	8·5
Ignition system		coil	coil	coil
Wheelbase (in.)	50	51·8	52·8	49·4
Seat height (in.)	26·8	28·3	27·6	27·2
Ground clearance (in.)	5·9	5·1	5·9	5·5
Dry weight (lb)	225	298	375	172

1) or 2 × 51·5.   2) or 347.   3) later 4·72.   4) option 3·50 × 19.

Country	Austria	Belgium		
Make	**Puch**	**FN**	**FN**	**Gillet**
Model	**800**	**M 12 SM**	**Tricar T3**	**720**
No. cylinders	4	2	2	2
Bore (mm)	60	90	90	76
Stroke (mm)	70	78	78	78
Capacity (cc)	792	992	992	708
Compression ratio (to 1)	5·0	5·0	5·0	5·75
Power: bhp	20	22	22	22
@ rpm	4000	4000	4000	4200

180

Country	Austria	Belgium		
Make	**Puch**	**FN**	**FN**	**Gillet**
Model	**800**	**M 12 SM**	**Tricar T3**	**720**
Valve type	sv	sv	sv	piston
No. gears	4	4+R	4+R	4+R
Top gear ratio	5·1			
Tyre (in.)	4·00 × 19	4·50 × 12	4·50 × 14	4·50 × 12
Brake (mm)		220	220	200
Front suspension	girder	girder	girder	girder
Rear suspension	rigid	rigid	elliptic	rigid
Petrol tank (litre)	17	19	19	17 or 20
Ignition system	coil	coil	coil	coil
Wheelbase (in.)	56·2			
Seat height (in.)	26·8			
Ground clearance (in.)	6·7	8·8	8·8	8·7
Dry weight (lb)	430	904	1433	882

Country	Belgium	Denmark	England	
Make	**Sarolea**	**Nimbus**	**AMC**	**AMC**
Model	**H**		**W39/G3**	**W41/G3L**
No. cylinders	2	4	1	1
Bore (mm)	88		69	69
Stroke (mm)	80		93	93
Capacity (cc)	973	750	348	348
Compression ratio (to 1)			6·3	5·9
Power: bhp		22		
Valve type	sv	ohc	ohv	ohv
No. gears	3+R × 2	3	4	4
Top gear ratio				5·8
Tyre (in.)	4·50 × 12			
Brake (mm)	200			
Front suspension	girder	teles	girder	teles
Rear suspension	rigid	rigid	rigid	rigid
Petrol tank (gal.)	4·8			3
Ignition system	coil	coil	magneto	magneto
Dry weight (lb)	1135			

Military Motorcycles of World War 2

Country	England			
Make	AMC	Ariel	Ariel	Ariel
Model	W40/G2D	W/NG	W/LG	W/VA
No. cylinders	1	1	1	1
Bore (mm)		72	61	81·8
Stroke (mm)		85	85	95
Capacity (cc)	250	346	248	499
Compression ratio (to 1)	7·0	6·5	6·0	
Power: bhp		17	12	
@ rpm	6000	5800	5400	
Valve type	ohv	ohv	ohv	sv
No. gears	4	4		4
Top gear ratio		5·7		
Front tyre (in.)		3·25 × 19		3·25 × 19
Rear tyre (in.)		3·25 × 19		3·25 × 19
Front suspension	girder	girder	girder	girder
Rear suspension	rigid	rigid	rigid	rigid
Petrol tank (gal.)		2·6		2·6
Ignition system	magneto	magneto		magneto
Dry weight (lb)	288	354		

Country	England			
Make	BSA	BSA	BSA	BSA
Model	M20	B30	C10	Twin
No. cylinders	1	1	1	2
Bore (mm)	82	71	63	62
Stroke (mm)	94	88	80	82
Capacity (cc)	496	348	249	495
Compression ratio (to 1)	4·9	7·2		5·8
Power: bhp	13			
@ rpm	4200			
Valve type	sv	ohv	sv	sv
No. gears	4	4	3	3
Top gear ratio	5·28			5·18
Front tyre (in.)	3·25 × 19			3·25 × 19
Rear tyre (in.)	3·25 × 19			3·25 × 19
Front brake (in.)	7	7		7
Rear brake (in.)	7	7		7
Front suspension	girder	girder	girder	teles
Rear suspension	rigid	rigid	rigid	rigid
Petrol tank (gal.)	3	3		2·5
Ignition system	magneto	magneto	coil	magneto
Wheelbase (in.)	54			54
Seat height (in.)	28·5			
Ground clearance (in.)	4·6			7
Dry weight (lb)	369			361 wet

Specifications

Country	England			
Make	Cotton	Douglas	James	Norton
Model			ML	350
No. cylinders	1	2	1	1
Bore (mm)		74	50	71
Stroke (mm)		70	62	88
Capacity (cc)	500	602	122	348
Compression ratio (to 1)		6·25	6·5	
Power: bhp			3	
@ rpm			4000	
Valve type	ohv	sv	piston	sv
No. gears	3 or 4	3	3	4
Top gear ratio		5·14	8·10	
Front tyre (in.)		3·25 × 19	2·75 × 19	
Rear tyre (in.)		3·50 × 19	2·75 × 19	
Front suspension	girder	leading link	girder	girder
Rear suspension	rigid	rigid	rigid	rigid
Petrol tank (gal.)		3		
Ignition system		magneto	fly. mag.	magneto
Wheelbase (in.)		53·5		
Dry weight (lb)		370 wet		

Country	England			
Make	Norton	Norton	Royal Enfield	Royal Enfield
Model	16H	Big 4	RE	D
No. cylinders	1	1	1	1
Bore (mm)	79	82	54	
Stroke (mm)	100	120	55	
Capacity (cc)	490	634	126	250
Compression ratio (to 1)	4·9	4·8		
Valve type	sv	sv	piston	sv
No. gears	4	4	3	
Top gear ratio	5·28	6·39		
Brake (in.)	7	7		
Front suspension	girder	girder	girder	girder
Rear suspension	rigid	rigid	rigid	rigid
Ignition system	magneto	magneto	fly. mag.	magneto

Country	England			
Make	Royal Enfield	Royal Enfield	Royal Enfield	Triumph
Model	C	CO	Twin	Generator
No. cylinders	1	1	2	2
Bore (mm)	70	70	52	63
Stroke (mm)	90	90	82	80
Capacity (cc)	346	346	348	499
Compression ratio (to 1)	5·0	5·75		

183

Military Motorcycles of World War 2

Country	England			
Make	Royal Enfield	Royal Enfield	Royal Enfield	Triumph
Model	C	CO	Twin	Generator
Power: bhp				15
@ rpm				4000
Valve type	sv	ohv	sv	ohv
No. gears	4	4	4	
Top gear ratio	5·95	5·65		
Rear tyre (in.)			4·50 × 17	
Front suspension	girders	girders	girders	
Rear suspension	rigid	rigid	rigid	
Petrol tank (gal.)				3
Ignition system	magneto	magneto	magneto	magneto
Dry weight (lb)				175 total

Country	England			
Make	Triumph	Triumph	Triumph	Triumph
Model	3SW	3HW	5SW	3TW
No. cylinders	1	1	1	2
Bore (mm)	70	70	84	
Stroke (mm)	89	89	89	
Capacity (cc)	343	343	493	350
Compression ratio (to 1)	5·3	6·7	5·6	
Power: bhp	12	17	15	17
@ rpm	4800	5200	4800	5400
Valve type	sv	ohv	sv	ohv
No. gears	4	4	4	3
Top gear ratio	6·1	5·78	4·95	5·89
Tyres (in.)	3·25 × 19	3·25 × 19	3·25 × 19	3·25 × 19
Brake (in.)	7	7	7	
Front suspension	girder	girder	girder	girder
Rear suspension	rigid	rigid	rigid	rigid
Petrol tank (gal.)	3·25	3·25	3·25	
Ignition system	magneto	magneto	magneto	magneto
Wheelbase (in.)	52·5	52·5	52·5	
Seat height (in.)	28·5	28·5	28·5	
Ground clearance (in.)	6	6	6	5
Dry weight (lb)	316	322	322	247[1]

1) later 263, all alloy 230.

Country	England			
Make	Triumph	Triumph	Velocette	Welbike
Model	5TW	TRW	MDD & MAF	
No. cylinders	2	2	1	1
Bore (mm)	63	63	68	50

Specifications

Country	England			
Make	Triumph	Triumph	Velocette	Welbike
Model	5TW	TRW	MDD & MAF	
Stroke (mm)	80	80	96	50
Capacity (cc)	499	499	349	98
Compression ratio (to 1)	5·0	6·0		6·0
Power: bhp		18		1·5
@ rpm		5000		
Valve type	sv	sv	ohv	piston
No. gears	4	4	4	1
Top gear ratio		5·8		
Front tyre (in.)		3·25 × 19		2·25 × 12·5
Rear tyre (in.)		4·00 × 19		2·25 × 12·5
Brake (in.)		7		
Front suspension	teles	teles	girder	rigid
Rear suspension	rigid	rigid	rigid	rigid
Petrol tank (gal.)		3		0·8
Ignition system	coil	magneto	magneto	fly. mag.
Wheelbase (in.)	52·5	53		39·5
Seat height (in.)		28·5		
Ground clearance (in.)		6.25		4·0
Dry weight (lb)	330	340		70

Country	France			Germany
Make	Gnome et Rhone	Rene Gillet	Rene Gillet	Ardie
Model	AX2			VF125
No. cylinders	2	2	2	1
Bore (mm)		70	80	51
Stroke (mm)		97·7	97·7	60
Capacity (cc)	804	752	982	123
Compression ratio (to 1)				6·75
Power: bhp				5
@ rpm				4500
Valve type	sv	sv	sv	piston
No. gears	4	4	4	3
Top gear ratio				9·2
Front tyre (in.)	3·50 × 19	27 × 4·00	27 × 4·00	2·50 × 19
Rear tyre (in.)	4·00 × 19	27 × 4·00	27 × 4·00	2·50 × 19
Front suspension	girder	leading link	leading link	girder
Rear suspension	rigid	rigid	rigid	rigid
Petrol tank (litre)				10·5
Ignition system	magneto	magneto	magneto	
Wheelbase (in.)				49·2
Seat height (in.)				26·4
Ground clearance (in.)				5·9
Dry weight (lb)				150

Military Motorcycles of World War 2

Country	Germany			
Make	**Ardie**	**BMW**	**BMW**	**BMW**
Model	**RBZ**	**R35**	**R4**	**R12**
No. cylinders	1	1	1	2
Bore (mm)	61	72	78	78
Stroke (mm)	66	84	84	78
Capacity (cc)	193	342	401	745
Compression ratio (to 1)	5·8	6·0	5·7	5·2
Power: bhp	7	14	12	18
@ rpm	5000	4500	3500	3400
Valve type	piston	ohv	ohv	sv
No. gears	3	4	4	4
Top gear ratio	6·6	5·63	5·11[1]	4·07[2]
Front tyre (in.)	3·00 × 19	3·00 × 19	26 × 3·5	3·00 × 19
Rear tyre (in.)	3·00 × 19	3·50 × 19	26 × 3·5	3·50 × 19
Front suspension	girder	teles	trailing link	teles
Rear suspension	rigid	rigid	rigid	rigid
Petrol tank (litre)	13·5	12	12	14
Ignition system		coil		magneto
Wheelbase (in.)	51·6			
Seat height (in.)	26·8			
Ground clearance (in.)	5·1			
Dry weight (lb)	262	342	302	409

1) later 5·63.   2) later 4·75.

Country	Germany			
Make	**BMW**	**BMW**	**BMW**	**BMW**
Model	**R75**	**R5**	**R61**	**R66**
No. cylinders	2	2	2	2
Bore (mm)	78	68	70	69·8
Stroke (mm)	78	68	78	78
Capacity (cc)	745	494	600	597
Compression ratio (to 1)	5·6	6·7	5·7	6·8
Power: bhp	26	24	18	30
@ rpm	4000	5800	4800	5300
Valve type	ohv	ohv	sv	ohv
No. gears	4 + R × 2	4	4	4
Top gear ratio	6·05[1]	3·89	3·89[2]	3·6[3]
Front tyre (in.)	4·50 × 16	3·00 × 19	3·00 × 19	3·00 × 19
Rear tyre (in.)	4·50 × 16	3·50 × 19	3·50 × 19	3·50 × 19
Front suspension	teles	teles	teles	teles
Rear suspension	rigid	rigid[4]	plunger	plunger
Petrol tank (litre)	24	15[5]	14	14
Ignition system	magneto	coil	coil	coil
Dry weight (lb)	926 with chair	364[6]	406	412

1) later 5·69.   2) later 4·62.   3) later 4·38.   4) R51 – plunger.   5) R51 – 14.   6) R51 – 401.

186

Country	Germany			
Make	BMW	DKW	DKW	DKW
Model	R71	RT 125	NZ 250	NZ 350
No. cylinders	2	1	1	1
Bore (mm)	78	52	68	72
Stroke (mm)	78	58	68	85
Capacity (cc)	745	123	247	346
Compression ratio (to 1)	5·5	6·0	5·9	5·7
Power: bhp	22	4·7	9	11·5
@ rpm	4600	4800	4000	4000
Valve type	sv	piston	piston	piston
No. gears	4	3	4	4
Top gear ratio	3·6[1]	7·85	5·2	4·2
Front tyre (in.)	3·00 × 19	2·50 × 19	3·00 × 19	3·25 × 19
Rear tyre (in.)	3·50 × 19	2·50 × 19	3·00 × 19	3·25 × 19
Front suspension	teles	girder	girder	girder
Rear suspension	plunger	rigid	rigid	rigid
Petrol tank (litre)	14	7·5	14	14
Ignition system	coil			
Wheelbase (in.)		48·4	53·1	53·1
Seat height (in.)		26·8	27·6	27·6
Ground clearance (in.)		5·9	4·7	4·7
Dry weight (lb)	412	150	298	320

[1] later 3·89.

Country	Germany			
Make	DKW	NSU	NSU	NSU
Model	NZ 500	251OS	601OSL	ZDB 125
No. cylinders	2	1	1	1
Bore (mm)	64	64	85	50
Stroke (mm)	76	75	99	62
Capacity (cc)	489	241	562	122
Compression ratio (to 1)	6·0	6·8	6·0	7·5
Power: bhp	18·5	10·5	24	4·8
@ rpm	4200	5000	5000	4500
Valve type	piston	ohv	ohv	piston
No. gears	4	4	4	3
Top gear ratio	4·3	6·4	5·0	7·9
Tyres (in.)	3·50 × 19	3·00 × 19	3·50 × 19	2·50 × 19
Front suspension	girder	girder	girder	girder
Rear suspension	plunger	rigid	rigid	rigid
Petrol tank (litre)	14	11·5	13·5	11
Wheelbase (in.)	56·7	50·4	57·5	50·4
Seat height (in.)	29·1	26·8	29·1	27·6
Ground clearance (in.)	5·5	4·3	5·1	5·1
Dry weight (lb)	430	300	408	181

Specifications

Military Motorcycles of World War 2

Country	Germany			
Make	NSU	TWN	Victoria	Zundapp
Model	HK 100	BD 250	KR35WH	DB 200
No. cylinders	4	1 split	1	1
Bore (mm)		2 × 45	69	60
Stroke (mm)		78	91·5	70
Capacity (cc)	1478	248	342	198
Compression ratio (to 1)		5·5	6·0	6·0
Power: bhp	36	11·2	18	7
@ rpm	3400	4000	5000	4000
Valve type	ohv	rotary	ohv	piston
No. gears	3+R × 2	4	4	3
Top gear ratio		5·1	5·3	5·8
Tyres (in.)	3·50 × 19	3·25 × 19	3·25 × 19	3·00 × 19
Front suspension	girder	girder	girder	girder
Rear suspension	tracks	rigid	rigid	rigid
Petrol tank (litre)	42	11·3	13	12
Ignition system	coil	coil	coil	coil
Wheelbase (in.)		52	55·9	51·2
Seat height (in.)		28·3	29·1	26·8
Ground clearance (in.)		4·3	5·1	5·1
Dry weight (lb)	2822	309	320	258

Country	Germany			
Make	Zundapp	Zundapp	Zundapp	Zundapp
Model	K500	K800	KS 600	KS 750
No. cylinders	2	4	2	2
Bore (mm)	69	62	75	75
Stroke (mm)	66·6	66·6	67·6	85
Capacity (cc)	498	804	597	751
Compression ratio (to 1)	5·8	5·8	6·5	6·2
Power: bhp	16	22	28	26
@ rpm	4800	4300	4700	4000
Valve type	sv	sv	ohv	ohv
No. gears	4	4	4	5+R
Top gear ratio	5·3	5·3	5·58	6·11
Tyres (in.)	3·50 × 19	3·50 × 19	3·50 × 19	4·50 × 16
Front suspension	girder	girder	girder	girder
Rear suspension	rigid	rigid	rigid	rigid
Petrol tank (litre)	12·5	12·5	15	23
Ignition system	coil	coil	coil	magneto
Wheelbase (in.)	54·7	55·3	55·5	55·9
Seat height (in.)	28·3	28·3	28·7	30·7
Ground clearance (in.)	5·1	4·7	5·1	6·3
Dry weight (lb)	397	425	430	882

Specifications

Country	**Italy**			
Make	**Benelli**	**Benelli**	**Bianchi**	**Gilera**
Model	**250**	**500**	**500**	**LTE**
No. cylinders	1	1	1	1
Bore (mm)	67	85		84
Stroke (mm)	70	87		90
Capacity (cc)	247	494	500	499
Compression ratio (to 1)				4·5
Power: bhp				10
@ rpm				3400
Valve type	ohc	ohc	ohc	sv
No. gears	4	4		4
Tyres (in.)				3·50 × 19
Front suspension	girder	girder	girder	girder
Rear suspension	s/a	s/a	s/a	s/a
Petrol tank (litre)				11
Ignition system	coil	coil		magneto
Dry weight (lb)				388

Country	**Italy**			
Make	**Gilera**	**Gilera**	**Moto Guzzi**	**Moto Guzzi**
Model	**Marte**	**Mercurio**	**GT17**	**Alce**
No. cylinders	1	1	1	1
Bore (mm)	84	84	88	88
Stroke (mm)	90	90	82	82
Capacity (cc)	499	499	499	499
Compression ratio (to 1)	5·0	5·5	4·7	4·7
Power: bhp	14	18	13·2	13·2
@ rpm	4800	4100	4000	4000
Valve type	sv	ohv	inlet sv exhaust ohv	inlet sv exhaust ohv
No. gears	4	4	3	4
Top gear ratio				5·32
Front tyre (in.)	3·50 × 19	4·50 × 17	3·50 × 19	3·50 × 19
Rear tyre (in.)	3·50 × 19	6·00 × 13	3·50 × 19	3·50 × 19
Front suspension	girder	girder	girder	girder
Rear suspension	s/a	semi-elliptic	s/a	s/a
Petrol tank (litre)	14	16	11·5	13·5
Ignition system	magneto	magneto	magneto	magneto
Wheelbase (in.)	55·1	87·4	59·8	57·3
Ground clearance (in.)				8·3
Length (in.)				87·4
Dry weight (lb)	660	1330	432	397

Military Motorcycles of World War 2

Country	Italy			
Make	Moto Guzzi	Moto Guzzi	Moto Guzzi	Moto Guzzi
Model	Trialce	GTS	Superalce	Mulo Meccanico
No. cylinders	1	1	1	2
Bore (mm)	88	88	88	80
Stroke (mm)	82	82	82	75
Capacity (cc)	499	499	499	754
Compression ratio (to 1)	4·7	4·7		6·5
Power: bhp	13·2	13·2	18·5	20
@ rpm	4000	4000	4300	4000
Valve type	inlet sv exhaust ohv	inlet sv exhaust ohv	ohv	ohv
No. gears	4 × 2	4	4	6 + R
Top gear ratio	6·53			
Front tyre (in.)	3·50 × 19	3·25 × 19	3·50 × 19	6·00 × 15
Rear tyre (in.)	3·50 × 19	3·50 × 19	3·50 × 19	6·00 × 15
Front suspension	girder	girder	girder	tele strut
Rear suspension	s/a	s/a	s/a	s/a
Petrol tank (litre)	16	12	12·5	53
Ignition system	magneto	magneto	magneto	
Wheelbase (in.)	74	55·1	57·3	
Ground clearance (in.)	8·3		8·3	
Length (in.)	111·2		87·4	
Dry weight (lb)	741	324	412	

Country	Italy			Japan
Make	Moto Guzzi	Moto Guzzi	Volugrafo	Rikuo
Model	Airone Militare	Motocarri ER	Aermoto	
No. cylinders	1	1	1	2
Bore (mm)	70	88		
Stroke (mm)	64	82		
Capacity (cc)	246	499	125	1200
Compression ratio (to 1)	6·0	5·5		
Power: bhp	9·5	17·8		28
@ rpm	4800	4300		
Valve type	ohv	ohv	piston	sv
No. gears	4	3	2 × 2	3 + R
Front tyre (in.)	3·00 × 19	3·50 × 19		4·75 × 18
Rear tyre (in.)	3·00 × 19	5·50 × 15		4·75 × 18
Front suspension	girder	girder	teles	bottom link
Rear suspension	s/a	semi elliptic	rigid	rigid
Petrol tank (litre)	11	16		
Ignition system	magneto	magneto	fly. mag.	
Wheelbase (in.)	53·9			
Dry weight (lb)	298	1058		

Specifications

Country	Sweden			
Make	m/42	m/42	NV	Suecia
Model	112 SV	112 TV		
No. cylinders	1	1	2	1
Bore (mm)	79	79	79	82
Stroke (mm)	101	101	101	94
Capacity (cc)	495	495	990	496
Compression ratio (to 1)	5·4	6·2		
Power: bhp	15·0	19·6[1]	36	
@ rpm	4000	4200[1]	4000	3600
Valve type	sv	ohv	ohv	sv
No. gears	3	3	6+R	4
Top gear ratio	5.33	5.05		
Tyres (in.)	3·50 × 19	3·50 × 19		
Brakes (mm)	185	185		
Front suspension	girder	girder	teles	girder
Rear suspension	rigid	plunger	rigid	rigid
Petrol tank (litre)	14	13·5		
Ignition system	magneto	magneto	magneto	coil
Wheelbase (in.)	55·9	55·5		55·9
Width (in.)	29·1	29·1		
Length (in.)	85·0	83·5		
Dry weight (lb)	397	441		364

1) 29·5/5500 with special cam

Country	USA			
Make	Harley-Davidson	Harley-Davidson	Harley-Davidson	Indian
Model	WLA	WLC	XA	640/741A
No. cylinders	2	2	2	2
Bore (in.)	2·75	2·75	3·062	2·5
Stroke (in.)	3·812	3·812	3·062	3·062
Capacity (cu. in.)	45·28	45·28	45·1	30·06
Compression ratio (to 1)	6·0		5·7	
Power: bhp	23			
@ rpm	4500			
Valve type	sv	sv	sv	sv
No. gears	3	3	4	3
Top gear ratio	4·6	4·6	4·7	
Tyres (in.)	4·00 × 18	4·00 × 18	4·00 × 18	3·50 × 18
Front suspension	bottom link	bottom link	bottom link	girder
Rear suspension	rigid	rigid	plunger	rigid
Petrol tank (gal.)	2·9	2·9	3·2	
Ignition system	coil	coil	coil	coil
Wheelbase (in.)	57·5		59·5	56·7
Ground clearance (in.)	4			5
Dry weight (lb)	540		565	450

Military Motorcycles of World War 2

Country	USA			
Make	**Indian**	**Indian**	**Indian**	**Simplex**
Model	**640B**	**340B**	**841**	
No. cylinders	2	2	2	1
Bore (in.)	2·875	3·25	2·875	
Stroke (in.)	3·5	4·437	3·5	
Capacity (cu. in.)	45·44	73·63	45·44	7·62
Power: bhp				4
@ rpm				4000
Valve type	sv	sv	sv	ported crank
No. gears	3	3	4	auto
Top gear ratio			5·1	belt
Front tyre (in.)	3·50 × 18	4·50 × 18		26 × 2·5
Front suspension	girder	trailing link	girder	bottom link
Rear suspension	rigid	plunger	plunger	rigid
Ignition system			coil	fly. mag.
Dry weight (lb)				125